THE TECH SALES
WARRIOR

THE **TECH SALES**
WARRIOR

CHRIS PRANGLEY

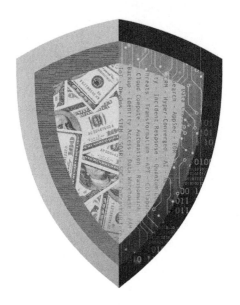

BATTLE-TESTED STRATEGIES
TO CRUSH QUOTA

LIONCREST
PUBLISHING

THE TECH SALES WARRIOR
Battle-Tested Strategies to Crush Quota

ISBN   978-1-5445-2747-5 *Hardcover*
          978-1-5445-2745-1 *Paperback*
          978-1-5445-2746-8 *Ebook*

To my parents—

who taught me the value of hard work,
believing in myself, and getting
back up after falling down.

CONTENTS

INTRODUCTION

EARLY IN MY CAREER, a company I worked for had gathered for its annual celebration on a cold January night in an elegant ballroom just off Times Square in New York City. It was the first time I'd attended the company's annual meeting; prior to that, I had been a business development rep—meaning my job had been to make cold call after cold call. But this past year I had been fast-tracked and promoted directly to an outside field rep.

I started off feeling good because it's the kind of event I love— everyone gets dressed up, there's a party atmosphere, and the positive mood of anticipation is irresistible. I chose a seat in the second row and couldn't wait for the awards ceremony to begin.

I had done "okay" as a field rep. I missed quota, but by less than 3 percent. For my first year, I thought that was awesome. I even had the idea that I might get some sort of award. But as they started calling people from my region of the country up on stage, it dawned

1

on me slowly at first, and then faster and faster, that I wasn't going to be called at all. My face felt hot. My stomach became a knot, my palms sweated, and my right leg bounced nervously. As I watched colleagues walk across the stage, basking in the cheers for nailing their yearly sales quota, I heard a voice next to me deliver crushing words.

"Prangley, they don't give out awards for trying here. I guess it's 'better luck next year' for you."

My mentor in the company, someone who had been helping guide my transition to a field rep, confirmed the final crushing blow of recognition: I had failed.

In that moment I learned one of the most important lessons in sales: you either meet quota or you don't. If you want to be up on stage and achieve financial freedom (and in some cases, keep your job), "okay" and "almost" won't cut it.

Now, before you jump to the conclusion that my mentor was some kind of sadist, you need to understand that he was teaching me an incredibly valuable lesson (and, okay, maybe needling me a bit).

There's no place to hide when you're a sales rep because the numbers are the numbers. In other words...

Everyone will know if you nailed it or failed it.

I think the best salespeople love the challenge this represents (or they learn to love it). These elite reps discover the Tech Sales Warrior mindset, and then go on to achieve financial freedom and a sense of accomplishment that is life altering.

I made it through the rest of the ceremony, and then it was out for drinks with colleagues. I made an effort to keep a smile on my face and socialize—after all, the people who met quota did deserve to be celebrated and congratulated. I certainly didn't want to be the sulking sore loser in the corner.

Even so, I couldn't help feeling like an imposter. A little bit of ribbing from colleagues about missing quota didn't help either. Some of it was good natured and some of it had more of an edge, but either way it added to my misery. If you've been in sales for any time at all, you probably know exactly the kind of teasing I'm talking about.

Eventually, I was able to slip away from this happy crowd of colleagues and head back to my hotel room. As I sat there alone, I recognized something inside me besides just disappointment and failure. It was the feeling of a fire being lit.

I wasn't sure exactly how yet, but I was absolutely determined: next year, I would be on that stage.

And I was. I never missed again. As devastating as those words from my mentor were, they would also mark the turning point of my sales career. The sting I felt fueled my determination to never miss quota again. With help, hard work, and learning from my own mistakes, I've since figured out how to crush quota consistently.

YOU CAN BE A TECH SALES WARRIOR

Learning to "crack the code" in tech sales has been life changing for me. If you're a new rep just starting out on your journey, the strategies I share in this book can be life transforming for you, too. It can also change the lives of reps who have been at it awhile, but haven't yet been able to break through to consistent success year after year.

I'm currently a regional vice president of sales for a leading, multi-billion-dollar cybersecurity firm, but I certainly didn't start there. Less than ten years ago, I was a new sales rep with a mountain of student loan debt and nagging worries about how to survive in the competitive world of tech sales.

In other words, I've been where you've been—maybe where you are. Some of my early sales experiences were a struggle, including that painful but memorable comment from my mentor as I watched other colleagues being celebrated on stage.

While I do believe the principles in this book can be applied successfully in other kinds of sales, this book is specifically aimed at B2B enterprise sales reps selling tech solutions.

It pains me to see tech sales reps trying but still feeling lost. I'm talking about the kind of reps who are disciplined and successful in other areas of their life, and aren't afraid of hard work, but somehow haven't been able to translate this into meeting quota consistently.

If you're one of these reps, this book will show you the methods, strategies, and tactics that are proven to work. If you bring the dedication and hard work, you'll learn how to channel your energy into the right tasks, the ones that produce results. It will pay off in financial freedom and the confidence that you're in control of your career.

I can say with absolute confidence these methods work. It's not just me they've worked for. I've mentored several young sales reps who've implemented these strategies and found consistent success. They are now Tech Sales Warriors, reliably exceeding quota.

You should wake up every single day with a mindset that matches the opportunity in front of you. Very few careers offer the earning potential of tech sales. The leading reps earn in the same stratosphere as the top doctors and top lawyers in the country. You can be up there with professional athletes and other fields that command top salaries.

Stop for a second and let that sink in. You can be compensated on the level of elite doctors, lawyers, and business leaders. It's a truly extraordinary opportunity that you should honor by bringing your best every day. If this fires you up, this book is for you. It will show you where to put your efforts and how to unlock your potential.

This Book Is Going to Bust Some Myths

There are some common misunderstandings about sales that are damaging if you allow yourself to buy into them. I'll go into more detail about these sales myths throughout the book, but recognizing these false ideas right from the start will put you a step ahead.

MYTH #1: It's All About Money

I've spent a good bit of this introduction talking about financial freedom and how you can make elite-level money. And now I seem to be saying the opposite, that it's a myth that sales is "all about money."

Let me explain. I've found that salespeople who focus exclusively on the "flash and cash"—who only want to make money for money's sake—flame out quickly. They either don't make it at all, or they meet quota a few times and then rapidly fade.

That's why the very first chapter of this book is called "Finding Your Why." If your goal is long-term success, you've got to have motivations that go beyond wanting to sit on a pile of money. When you have a deeper purpose, it'll fuel you through the mundane tasks and frequent rejection that are an inevitable part of sales.

MYTH #2: Sales Is about Tricking People

Of all the misconceptions about sales, this one drives me the craziest. Great salespeople are not manipulators. They're not tricksters looking to deceive someone into buying. The most successful salespeople build relationships and truly care about what's best for their prospective clients.

Most importantly, extraordinary salespeople want to deliver tremendous value for clients. Sales should always be a win-win, with the customer getting a painful problem solved or reaping significant financial benefits from the solution you sell.

The goal is never to be slick or deceptive. The goal should always be to deliver value.

MYTH #3: There's a Lot of Luck Involved in Beating Quota

This is a crippling mindset for any sales rep to have. It implies that meeting quota is out of your hands. This is an especially persistent false belief because sometimes luck *does* play a role in particular circumstances.

I've seen reps luck into one massive sale that makes their year. And I've seen good deals fall apart near the end when the rep did everything right. I've seen reps with "great" accounts fail, and I've seen reps with the "worst" accounts still crush quota. Good and bad luck happens.

But luck is not decisive over the course of a career. It's not even the determining factor in meeting quota in any given year. If you do the work and follow these methods, you can consistently crush quota, year after year. Some years you'll have more good fortune than others. But all that will mean is you'll exceed quota by even more than you usually do.

The Warrior Mindset

I've always been a big fan of self-help and self-development advice. I've taken advantage of all kinds of resources and I'm grateful for the ones that have helped me enormously on my journey.

But there are two potential downsides to self-development guides that I want to help you avoid. First, stay away from any self-help guru who promises quick fixes. The "easy solutions" mindset is the exact opposite of the one you need.

Here's the unavoidable reality: many of your daily tasks are going to be a grind. This is especially true at the beginning of a career when you're trying to build every relationship from scratch. This book will help you find the fun in sales (there's lots of it). But there's no getting around that you'll need a warrior mindset. If you don't have one already, I'll give you some methods for finding it. If you're already a warrior, I'll give you ways to strengthen and reinforce that attitude.

The second problem with self-help resources is this: too many people consume them, feel good about it for a few hours, and then never do anything with it. This book does not come with magic pills that you can swallow and become instantly successful. I'm talking about quality advice that you know you should be implementing, not the quick fix stuff. You must take action, and it will be hard work. If you're ready to do that, this book holds the key to a genuinely amazing opportunity.

Warriors apply what they learn, and they do that over and over and over. Warriors never stop looking for ways to improve.

It's Okay to Get Excited—This Stuff Works!

Here's my final thought for getting the most out of this book: read it with confidence and hope.

Possibly you've picked up this book because you want to make enough money to wipe out student debt, eliminate chronic money concerns, and support family and friends financially.

And you're probably yearning for the feeling of accomplishment that comes with consistent success.

Or maybe you have a fire inside that makes you want all of that and more.

This book has what you need to get where you want to go. Read. Apply. And I'll see you on the stage.

CHAPTER 1

FINDING YOUR WHY

"I learned this, at least, by my experiment;
that if one advances confidently in the direction of
his dreams, and endeavors to live the life which
[he] has imagined, [he] will meet with a
success unexpected in common hours."

—Henry David Thoreau

A FEW YEARS BACK, I was driving to a sales event and I picked up a young sales rep on the way.

As he got in my car, he said, "You're driving a Honda, Prangley?"

"Yeah, a Honda."

"I'm sorry to hear that," he said with a grin.

At the time, I had been exceeding quota for a few years and could have owned a showier car, but my preference at the time was to save and build toward a completely secure future. Besides, I like Hondas.

The grinning young man had an entry-level position as an inside sales rep, making in the neighborhood of $60,000 to $90,000 a year. But his current car was a fully loaded Alfa Romeo.

As he chuckled at me, I just smiled pleasantly and thought, "We'll see."

The attitude of this young person is one I've seen many times in tech sales (although admittedly he was an extreme example). His Instagram was full of pictures projecting a rich lifestyle, and he was caught up in the "'flash and cash" idea of sales.

Tech sales is genuinely lucrative. There are many sales reps making well into six figures (and even seven figures in a particularly good year). The sales themselves can be in the millions. All this can be heady stuff for a young person who wants "in on it."

But I've noticed some reps miss a big part of the success equation: hard work. It's not slick talk or projecting a lifestyle that gets the job done; you've got to put in sweat equity. That means early mornings and late nights, and making sacrifices for a better future.

You definitely can build your way to fantastic earnings and even do it relatively quickly. With hard work and a compounding effect, huge earnings within three years is realistic. The key is having a warrior mentality toward the day-to-day work, plus a mindset focused on the long term. That's how you build a career.

But instead, I see too many young reps who think, "I'm going to grab as much as I can as fast as I can, and this is going to be easy." That was unfortunately the attitude of the rep driving the Alfa Romeo (and I'll tell you what happened to him at the end of this chapter).

If you're truly serious about building a fantastic career, it needs to be built on the proper foundation. And the key to that is "Finding Your Why."

Finding Your Why is about discovering your deep statement of purpose. It's something that is unique and personal to you.

I'm going to give you some specific guidance on how to do this, but first I need to tell you why this step is so crucial. Some of you may be tempted to either skip this step or treat it like a quick, shallow exercise. But Finding Your Why is not something you brainstorm for thirty minutes, pick out something that sounds good, and then you're ready to go. That's not even close to deep enough.

Your Why has to power you through grinding days packed with cold call after cold call; your Why has to push you through a ton of rejection; and your Why needs to motivate you to dedicate the time and effort necessary to beat quota, even on days when you're not feeling it.

It's just too difficult to stand up to the tougher aspects of sales if your Why is not deeply connected to who you are as a person. It must align with your core motivation and values. The first rule of Finding Your Why is not to rush it.

Some might be skeptical about the emphasis I'm putting on Finding Your Why. I can hear these doubters saying, "Hey, I want to make money; it's not about some deeper purpose. Can't you just teach me the nuts and bolts of complex B2B tech sales and skip all this intangible stuff?"

Fair question, and this book will most definitely cover the nuts and bolts you'll need. However, I can tell you from my own experience and observing others: you WILL burn out if your only Why is "I want to make money." It might happen in six months, or it might take a few years, but without connecting to a deeper motivation, you'll eventually find yourself failing to push through the mundane tasks and regular rejection that is an inevitable part of sales.

Once you grasp the motivational power of having a Why, you need to take practical steps to figure out what that deep purpose is for you.

Tips, Tricks, and Traps of "Finding Your Why"

A Why is not something you pick from a menu of preapproved choices. And I can't give you a mathematical formula or an exact recipe that will inevitably produce a fundamental purpose. It's not an "insert tab A into slot B" type thing.

What I can do is give you guidelines and practical advice on how to find it. If you put in sincere effort, you will discover it. This is an ongoing process, and you must avoid the trap of impatience. Commit to doing the deep work and taking whatever time is needed. Believe me, you will NEVER regret spending time getting this right. It will be the foundation for your success.

So, where do you start? Here are some questions to launch your quest to find your own personal Why:

- What is it that you genuinely want out of your life?

- Who's important to you in your life?

- What belief or activity or goal would get you out of bed every single morning with a fury of energy and thankfulness?

- Is there an idea or principle that you find incredibly motivating?

Do not rush through these questions! A best practice is to do some journaling. Put on a playlist of relaxing music, sit down, and give yourself the freedom to explore.

It's helpful to keep in mind this process is very personal. As you think through it, remember there's no requirement to share any of it with anyone (unless of course you want to). Be completely honest with yourself and truly give yourself the freedom to explore your deepest motivations. Don't censor yourself or look for someone else's answer. Find yours.

Let me open up a bit about my own experience so you can see what I mean. When I was struggling to find my own Why, I thought a lot about financial freedom. I wanted to be successful, and I didn't want to have chronic worries about money.

It might sound at first like "financial freedom" is a good purpose. But it wasn't enough. There was a moment where I said to myself, "I'm showing up and doing what I'm supposed to do on paper, but there's something missing here."

The problem was this: when you examine it closely, "financial freedom" is too vague to be useful. After all, who would say that they don't want financial freedom? If it's that general, it's not a true Why.

My vague Why transformed into deep motivation when I had an

insight about what significant financial success would mean for me. It would mean I could have the resources to be able to help family and friends. That I could be an anchor for others and be able to help generously and without worry.

Of course, that doesn't mean that I don't enjoy the material benefits financial freedom allows in my own life; it's certainly a part of my motivation. But it wasn't until I tied it to something greater than myself that I found my true core inspiration. Once I found that, everything clicked into place and I had the fuel I needed to power through my days. It changed everything for me and supercharged my daily motivation.

Please don't read this as saying you should have the same Why or that it always has to be fundamentally other directed to be a powerful motivator (although I do believe many powerful Whys come from what we can do for others).

I give you the above example from my own experience to point you in the right direction, not to hand you your own Why. You'll need to figure that out for yourself because no one can do it for you.

To give you more food for thought, here are some examples of deeply purposeful Whys:

- I was born to serve others and help people overcome challenges.

- By helping other firms solve their own problems, I will be able to provide for my family.

- Through my natural gifts of selling, I can provide for those less fortunate.

- I was born to help companies grow by delivering massive value to others.

- I'm a natural leader who is willing to fail, learn, and grow no matter the challenge.

While I recommend having a single Why statement, it can be useful to supplement your deep purpose with a list of personal, spiritual, and/or financial goals. Having some clearly defined goals aligned with your Why can keep the fire burning.

Here are some examples of those kinds of concrete goals:

- Pay off my mortgage before forty.

- Surprise my mom with a trip to Paris to show appreciation for everything she has done for me.

- Support a family in the community through the holidays.

- Pay off my student loans in a year.

- Give back to the schools that gave so much to me.

- Travel to the most exotic place in the world and learn about a new culture.

- Go on adventures of a lifetime that I otherwise wouldn't be able to afford.

- Buy the boat, car, or house of my dreams.

- Pay for my kids' education so they don't have to go through what I did.

Once you have your Why, and your goals, should you proclaim it for all the world to hear, or should you keep it private?

In my experience, there's no single right answer that fits everyone. If sharing it widely and posting it prominently in your work area motivates you, do it.

If you think of it as deeply personal and private motivation, then by all means keep it to yourself. Some people find a happy medium by sharing it with those closest to them.

Before and After "Finding Your Why"

Here's what finding my deep purpose did for me. Early in my sales career, I had goals about retiring some significant student loan debt and getting some financial breathing room. I was doing reasonably well, putting in the work, but something still wasn't completely clicking. I wanted more out of myself, but the fire in the belly wasn't 100 percent lit.

My self-talk sounded something like this: "I'm showing up and doing what I'm supposed to do on paper, but there's something missing here." I started reading self-help books, journaling, and seeking other resources, and that's when I realized I needed to go deeper inside myself to find my true motivation.

RECOMMENDED RESOURCES

There have been many books that have impacted my Why, as well as my goal setting, clarity of mind, and successful habit creation. Here are some I highly recommend:

1. On the value of controlling your future by taking ownership of your thoughts and your daily output,

I recommend *Awaken the Giant Within* by **Tony Robbins**. It was absolutely foundational for my success in business. Key quote: "Anytime you sincerely want to make a change, the first thing you must do is raise your standards."

2. On controlling your thoughts and attitude and finding new power through affirmations and faith, read *The Power of Positive Thinking* by **Norman Vincent Peale** and *You Can't Afford the Luxury of a Negative Thought* by **John-Roger and Peter McWilliams**.

3. To help awaken yourself to universal truths in simple words, and to learn to use logic to overcome difficult situations, read philosophy (especially the Stoics, and early Platonic and Aristotelian philosophers). Key quote: "Dripping water hollows out stone not through force, but through persistence." —Ovid

4. On the power of using imagination and faith to overcome any obstacle and push forward with your mission, read *Think and Grow Rich* by **Napoleon Hill**. Key quote: "When faith is blended with

the vibration of thought, the subconscious mind instantly picks up the vibration, translates it into its spiritual equivalent, and transmits it to Infinite Intelligence, as in the case of prayer."

5. For understanding that you are unique, have a calling, and no one else on this planet can do what you have been called to do, read ***Man's Search for Meaning* by Viktor E. Frankl**. It will help you seek meaning and your Why, even through the most extreme events. Key quote: "Everyone has his own specific vocation or mission in life to carry out a concrete assignment which demands fulfillment."

6. On the importance of systems and habits, read ***Atomic Habits: An Easy and Proven Way to Build Good Habits & Break Bad Ones* by James Clear**. Without strong habits, you won't meet your goals. You need to implement systems to achieve your goals. Key quote: "You do not rise to the level of your goals. You fall to the level of your systems."

7. On mastery, thinking long term, and embracing the day-to-day process, read ***Mastery: The Keys to Success and Long-Term Fulfillment* by George**

Leonard. Key quote: "There's a seemingly endless road ahead of you with numerous setbacks along the way and—most important—plenty of time on the plateau, where long hours of diligent practice gain you no apparent progress at all."

8. On taking ownership of your life, your past and circumstances, and your future success by focusing exclusively on your own actions and thoughts, read *As a Man Thinketh* **by James Allen**. It reinforces the idea that no outside person, past, or situation is the reason to blame for falling short. Key quote: "Man is buffered by circumstances so long as he believes himself to be the creature of outside conditions, but when he realizes that he is a creative power, and that he may command the hidden soil and seeds of his being out of which circumstances grow, he then becomes the rightful master of himself."

9. On the power of using Morning Pages to brain dump, clear the mind, and develop an effective strategy for personal and creative growth, read *The Artist's Way* **by Julia Cameron**.

Once I found that I wanted to be that financial anchor for the people in my life, my whole perspective changed. I was doing many of the same things I was doing before, but now with more gusto and more joy. Going in early was no longer a chore. The cold calls, the working lunches, the evening hours—none of that seemed so bad anymore.

To this day, I still remind myself of my Why on days when I need that extra fuel or if things aren't going well.

Finding your deep purpose also helps create momentum. Think of it as an endless positive feedback loop that drives you to higher and higher levels of success. Your motivation pushes you to be the first one at the office and the last one to leave whenever you need to put in additional work to get a deal done. It helps you make those extra cold calls and spend time crafting emails that get results. That leads to breakthrough success, which in turn reinforces your positive feelings toward your purpose.

The bottom line is this: you'll never regret the time you spend Finding Your Why.

Testing Your Why

The true test of your statement is whether or not it fuels you. If you think you found your purpose but after a short time realize you're still just going through the motions, you haven't nailed it yet.

There's no need to panic or think that you'll never find it. Remember, this is not a quick exercise. Set aside some more time and return to journaling. Maybe you need to change its fundamental orientation. If your Why is inner directed, explore a purpose that is motivated toward helping others. Or vice versa. Change it up and see what clicks.

Whatever you do, don't get discouraged if your first try at a Why failed. Feeling tense or in a rush is a sure way to block the thoughts and feelings you need to uncover. Relax and it will happen.

However long it takes you, don't give up—it's too important. The foundation for a great career in tech sales is having a deep purpose. You cannot have a warrior mentality without it.

I did promise to tell you what happened to the young man with the Alfa Romeo. Unfortunately, less than six months after that day I gave him a ride to the sales event, he was let go for underperforming. Not everyone is cut out for sales, and I certainly hope he found a career that is happy and fulfilling for him. But I do think it is a good reminder to not focus exclusively on money and lifestyle. No one has ever built a career in sales by projecting the right image on Instagram. You have to do the work.

It's also a great reminder that Finding Your Why is crucial. Instead of focusing on fancy cars right off the bat, be a warrior who learns to love the struggle, and meet it head-on with a deep purpose. When you do that, you'll discover that fancy cars, amazing vacations, and a beautiful home will all come with time.

ACTION STEPS FOR CHAPTER 1:

- Set aside serious time for Finding Your Why.

- Journaling is highly recommended. Explore ideas on paper in a relaxing atmosphere. Put on some music if that helps you reflect and cut out all distractions.

- Be patient and don't necessarily grasp at the first thing that sounds good.

- Once you have a Why, test it. Is it truly motivating you or are you still struggling to feel excited about what you're doing? If you're still struggling, go back and do some more journaling. You'll get there.

- Decide whether this is going to be something you keep private or if it is something you post in your work area for all to see. Either is fine; do what makes you most comfortable.

- Create concrete goals that align with your purpose. Implement habits to ensure you achieve those goals.

- Meaning in your work and a purpose for your life will drive you through hardship and give you an unwavering energy to tackle new challenges.

CHAPTER 2

YOU ARE A BRAND

"Don't let others define you.
Define yourself."

—Virginia M. Rometty

THERE ARE MORE THAN 200,000 tech companies that sell software, hardware, or IT services in the US.

Stop and think about how many sales positions there must be with more than a quarter of a million companies in the marketplace. If you're ever doubtful that there are plentiful opportunities, remember this number. It's incredibly energizing to realize how many tech sales jobs there are.

However, the flip side must be acknowledged. With that many companies and jobs, there must be a sizable number that are a bad match for you. Choosing your opportunities wisely is crucial to having a successful career.

This chapter is about how to effectively navigate those career choices. But before you can do that, you first need to understand the importance of thinking of yourself as a brand. Once you grasp this concept, you'll be in a much better position to figure out the companies you'd like to work for.

YOU ARE A BRAND

What is a brand?

At the most fundamental level, a brand tells the story of the company. Maybe the story the company wants to tell is that they have the friendliest customer experience, or the most cutting-edge products, or their solutions provide the best value.

So, first and foremost, a company wants its brand to express the company's story consistently.

The other thing companies want to do with their brand is protect it. Companies vigorously guard the reputation of their brand. Letting standards slip or doing something unethical can undermine the brand story and damage the company.

Your job is to think of yourself as a brand and have the exact same goals as a company. You should be telling a consistent story about yourself through your interactions with everyone. And you need to keep your reputation intact by maintaining high standards for conduct, both practical and ethical.

This might seem a little far afield from choosing a company to work for, but I promise it connects. Stick with this detour just a bit longer and it all will become clear.

What actions matter when you are creating your own personal brand? Here are some examples:

- How fast you respond to emails and phone calls.

- Your clothes and your personal grooming.

- The level of your preparation for meetings.

- Always doing what you tell people you're going to do.

- Your attention to detail when responding to a request.

This kind of list could go on for pages, and that's the point. Building your brand is about being mindful of how ALL your interactions are impacting others. Every action you take is a chance to add positively to your brand or to hurt it. My advice is to channel the mentality of a warrior and be relentless in pursuing excellence in all your dealings.

Being a brand unto yourself is not just about attention to detail and conscientious follow-up. You need real skills as part of your brand. So figure out how to improve your presentations. Find out how to become better at client research. Get advice on how to better connect with prospects.

The good news is this book can help with all of that. But you should never stop with one book. There's no shortage of resources and strategies if you're willing to make improving your own brand a priority. I've used every one of the resources and strategies on the following list. You should, too:

- Books (but avoid anything that promises success without hard work).

- Podcasts.

- Review industry websites, including competitors, conferences, articles about your space, and adjacent technology.

- Attend trade shows.

- Find mentors, including standout sales reps and company managers.

- Shadow leading performers.

- Ask for direct feedback after presenting. You can also record yourself to understand how you come across.

- Monitor how prompt you are to meetings. Are you always on time, or do you find yourself making excuses for being late on a regular basis?

- Ask ten close friends for honest feedback on your appearance and dress, and what image you project. Is there anything they recommend? Look for the common response among the feedback, not the outlier.

- Hire a coach. Examples of types of coaches to consider: stylist, speaking, writing, negotiation, meditation/prayer, nutritionist, physical trainer, improv, or anything else that can make you better.

The key is this: get passionate about building your brand. I promise you the rewards will be amazing.

Okay, end of detour. Now we're finally ready to circle back and talk about finding the right place to work.

The companies you work for over the course of your career are where you execute your own personal brand strategy. You can't succeed in building your own brand in the wrong setting.

When you find a company that's the right fit for you, your brand will be enhanced by the association with the company. The right company is also the kind of place that gives you the opportunity to improve your brand by developing more skills.

While this book is not an in-depth job-hunting guide, I do think it could be helpful to give you a basic framework for finding the right job for you. And if you already have a current tech sales job, I'll give you some things to think about before deciding to change companies.

As was noted at the top of this chapter, there are A LOT of tech companies. The first thing you need to do is narrow it down to a small subset of them that you want to target. Otherwise, the process is pretty much unmanageable.

A good place to start narrowing is to think about what kind of tech solution you want to sell. There's infrastructure, cybersecurity, HR software, business analytics, data management, collaboration tools, and much more. What technology excites you?

Maybe you want to explore some of the collaboration products out there that help global companies connect both internally and externally. Perhaps the idea of stopping cyberattacks that can cost companies millions is something that interests you. Or possibly you want to sell an HR solution that helps clients make their employee experience more enjoyable and efficient.

Then within each niche, there are sub niches where you can narrow your choices, like specializing in secure web gateways (SWG) within the overall niche of cybersecurity.

Another option is to be more of a generalist and work for a reseller and system integrator that handles many different kinds of tech solutions for clients. Whether you become a specialist or generalist, the main thing is to find something you can be excited to present to clients.

Once you have an area you're interested in, you next want to consider company size. Think about the differences between small, medium, and large companies, and reflect on what size best matches your personality. Startups are another kind of company to consider. There are always plenty of those in the tech space.

Large companies tend to have lots of opportunities and numerous career paths, but some people prefer the work environment of small- or medium-size companies. There's absolutely nothing wrong with wanting to be a big fish in a small pond. The benefits to each option are numerous, but the opportunities to get promoted will be easier in middle-sized companies, as opposed to the bureaucracy of a large corporation with hundreds of thousands of employees.

Maybe the energy and risk of a startup gets you fired up. There can be big rewards, of course, but also more potential downside than with an established company. If you're interested in a startup, I do recommend you research how promising their products are and how good the leadership is. The leadership team of a startup is crucial for success, so make sure you're comfortable that they know what they're doing.

Now it's time to circle back to the concept of you as a brand. As you contemplate what kind of company you want to work for, always put it in the context of the brand you want to build for yourself. Which kind of company will best match your long-range vision for who you are as a brand?

I do want to provide an extra word of advice here. There is one kind of company I usually recommend avoiding when building a career. In every tech market, there are always the cheaper players. Do you want to spend your time chasing the cheapest clients, offering bargain-basement prices, with meager support deployment and threadbare customer service?

Here's an example from the world of cybersecurity. It's safe to say every company needs a firewall or a version of an antivirus software, and there are many tech companies looking to sell them fast and easy. It's a more straightforward process, and in some cases the sales approach is more about hope than strategy. There are some new innovators in these spaces, but if you choose to work for one of the traditional players, you won't be learning much about the strategy and execution of complex sales. The go-to market for some of these companies is to chase the next renewal or drop to the lowest price.

This type of sales job will hold you back for two reasons. One, you're not developing the skills you need to close complex B2B tech sales and that hurts your career growth potential. Secondly, if you go with a dinosaur firm or a very cheap alternative, you're harming your brand, because working for one of these companies speaks volumes about the kind of rep you want to be and the sales style you've been practicing.

Once you have all the criteria you want to use to find the right company for you, the next question is this: how do you go about locating the best potential employers?

One thing I recommend is reading *The Wall Street Journal*. You can easily search their online edition by plugging in whatever tech niche you're interested in. Notice the companies that are being mentioned and start there with your research.

You can also monitor the Nasdaq and NYSE to identify consistent, strong, and reliable brands. You'll learn who's growing, who's struggling, what are the trends in the space, and more.

Other sources of information are Gartner and Forrester. Both have extensive databases that contain a treasure trove of solid information about niche markets, company size, customer reviews, and other important data. The most obvious resource is, of course, Google search. You definitely can find some great information, but always be cautious to consider the source of any article you click on. Google does offer a great way to springboard into a niche and find other leading, private companies or new innovators that you wouldn't otherwise find watching the stock market.

Glassdoor, a review site for employees to share what it's like to work for a company, is also a good resource. But take what you learn with a grain of salt. Many negative reviews are from people who likely weren't cutting it as salespeople and that frustration comes out in the review. It's best to look for consistent feedback over time rather than a few angry reviews.

There are also a plethora of tech magazines, business publications, and online resources to learn more about technology niches, trends, products, investments in tech firms, and more. Some of these include *CIO* magazine, CSO Online, Forbes Technology Council, *Wired* magazine, CNBC, *Bloomberg Businessweek* magazine, *MIT Technology Review*, *Financial Times*, TechCrunch.com, ZDNET.com, *SC Magazine*, Dark Reading, Network Computing, and *Computer World*. Seek the technology sector that excites you to make an impact in people's lives.

I do want to emphasize the importance of LinkedIn. It's a great place to do some research about a company, particularly if you can find some common connections who work for companies you're interested in. Use those connections to reach out directly to find out more about what it's like to work there (tactfully, of course). I know firsthand how valuable it can be because it helped me get my first job in tech sales when I didn't know a soul at the company I reached out to. Your school's alumni page may even help you with organic introductions, so leverage that option, too.

One other word about LinkedIn. I sometimes see people treat it like every other social media platform, and that's a mistake. This isn't Facebook, so be extra mindful of what you post. Keep everything professional, engage with your network, and keep it updated. (LinkedIn is also a valuable prospecting tool and that will be covered in a later chapter.) The key thing to remember is that LinkedIn is a primary place to showcase your brand. Don't blow it by posting or commenting anything unprofessional.

Be careful of anything you share or publish about companies in the industry you serve. For example, if you sell in the cybersecurity space, don't share or publish damaging remarks on LinkedIn, Twitter, any other social platform, or in email outreach about companies that have been breached. It's easy to reshare an article or chime in with a snarky comment on something in the moment, but it destroys your trust and reputation when that company is seeking a solution like yours to help them. Why would a firm turn to someone who badmouthed them in the public eye or used their loss as a marketing ploy? Think long term. Warren Buffett said it best: "It takes twenty years to build a reputation and five minutes to ruin it. If you think about that you'll do things differently."

Once you start applying to your target companies, find ways to stand out. You should personalize the outreach by doing a little specific research on the company and the person you're reaching out to. Find ways to provide value, highlight your commitment, share how you align with the role, and demonstrate that you've done your homework.

SHOULD I STAY OR SHOULD I GO?

If you already have a tech sales job, how do you weigh staying versus looking for other opportunities?

First, look at your current position through the lens we've been referencing throughout this chapter. Is your current company one that matches your brand? Can you develop here, and if you do eventually decide to leave, will it look good on your résumé?

If the answer to one or both of these is a definite no, then move on as soon as you can.

However, if the issue is not with the opportunity at the company, but more about the fact that you're struggling, here's what I suggest.

First, finish reading this book and implement the concepts. You may find that you'll start closing more sales and what looked like a dead end is suddenly a wonderful job.

Second, be proactive in reaching out to others in your company. It's usually well known internally who the top sales performers in the company are. Ask them if you can have a few minutes of their time and pick their brains about what you can be doing differently. You may even find it leads to a mentoring relationship. I need to emphasize that you should look for the salespeople who have consistently done well over time, not someone who just happened to have a couple of good quarters.

You can also turn to your manager and be honest about your struggles. Open up and ask what you can be doing to get better. The response to this is almost always positive. In the occasional case where you may have a manager who is problematic, look for ways to reach out to other managers in the company for advice, using tact and discretion of course.

In general, I find many people are too quick to leave a company and tend to have a "the grass is greener over the next hill" mentality. Always carefully consider how leaving will work for or against your brand. If you jump around too much, that won't look good on your résumé or LinkedIn profile. You also may find yourself starting over again and again, instead of building a career for the long haul.

If you're a person who jumps ship every two years or so, that will have a massive negative impact on your earning potential because you'll constantly be in the state of rebuilding. Remember that nothing great happens overnight. I recently worked with a rep who was out for months on maternity leave, yet still brought in hundreds of thousands of dollars in deals. That isn't luck; it's a system and something she had built over time.

I worked with another rep who has been above 120 percent of quota for the past three years in a row (on a multimillion-dollar annual number) and on his fourth year of success is currently at over 200 percent of his annual number with half a year to go. Once again, this isn't luck; this is a system of success rooted in a long-term approach to growth. To make the most money and have the most success in your career, you have to invest in yourself and your company for the long haul. When you think long term, invest long term, and do consistent work, you'll create a system of success, not luck.

Unsure still? That's okay, keep giving it some thought. In the meantime, let's move to the next chapter, which can be the most life-changing chapter in the book if you let it.

ACTION STEPS FOR CHAPTER 2:

- Always keep the "You Are a Brand" concept firmly in your mind. For every decision and action related to work, ask yourself, "Is this helping or hurting my brand?"

- You also need to always remember that no one is going to care about your career as much as you do. It's up to you to develop your skills and your brand or it won't happen.

- Set aside some time each week outside of working hours for self-development through books, seminars, coaching, and other resources. Book it in your calendar so it actually happens.

- Decide whether your current position fits your brand. If it does, write down a list of potential mentors at your company to reach out to. Commit to implementing the concepts in this book and start crushing it in your current position.

- If you need a job or need to change jobs, go through the tips in this chapter to narrow it down to a target list of companies. As you go deeper into the process, make sure the companies you're aiming for match your brand and will tell a good story on your résumé.

- Seek out what fires you up and what you're passionate about. Your love for your work, for your career, and for your customers will shine against your competition.

CHAPTER 3

NO ONE EVER MET THEIR QUOTA IN ONE DAY

"For this reason, your energy
should go into building better habits,
not chasing better results."

—James Clear

AS AN OUTSIDE FIELD REP in the world of enterprise sales, your daily habits are worth somewhere between $1.4 million and $6.4 million above your normal earnings over a twenty-year period. And that's probably an underestimate.

Find that hard to believe?

Here are the numbers to back it up. Let's say you've been an outside rep for a few years and your base salary is $90,000. And then, assuming you just barely hit quota but don't exceed it significantly, you'll get an additional $90,000 for hitting your goal (your "on track earnings" [OTE]). That's $180,000. Not bad, but you left money on the table. A lot of money. And you probably had to deal with a lot of anxiety all year because you were constantly worried about whether you'd hit quota.

If you only hit quota, what did you miss out on? You missed accelerated bonuses that will push you into new income brackets and change your life; you missed pushing yourself to the potential you have within; you likely also missed President's Club recognition (bragging rights); and all of the other benefits that come from being a top performer at your company (stock, pay bumps, choices, advancement, and a strong personal brand).

If you had followed a system that allowed you to reliably exceed quota, it's extremely doable to begin averaging $250,000 to $500,000 a year ($90,000 base + $90,000 standard bonus for hitting OTE, and then additional commission of somewhere between $70,000 to $320,000). I know this is possible because I've used this system to do it, and I've seen others do the same.

Of course, your base and incentives may vary from this example, and will also probably change over the course of your career. Keep in mind that your OTE will eventually stop rising as you hit industry ceilings. (If you ask colleagues that have been at it for ten to twenty years, they'll confirm that.) Once you hit those maximums, the only way to make more money is to crush quota and nail the money accelerators we're talking about.

Let's be extremely conservative with our numbers and say your career is twenty years long. If you average $250,000 instead of $180,000, that's an additional $70,000 a year, or $1.4 million over your career. If you average $500,000, that's an additional $320,000 a year, or $6.4 million over those twenty years.

I want to emphasize that these are not "pie-in-the-sky" numbers, but achievable figures for those who follow a system of daily prospecting. Some years will no doubt be better than others, but the averages will hold up if you're consistent.

Two other benefits should be noted here. The additional $1.4 million to $6.4 million is just a calculation of additional earnings, but if you're investing even a fraction of these extra bonuses, the rewards go up even more.

Here is another benefit, and in a way it's priceless: you can stop chronically worrying about just barely meeting quota. You'll also stop being a person who has the mindset of just doing the minimums, and become stronger and better in the process. With discipline and habit, you'll learn more about yourself, grow into the person you want to be, and live an extremely fulfilling life. Instead of passing time or leaning on hope, you can look forward to seeing how far you'll exceed your goals every year and how it will impact your growth as a person.

To put it in the simplest terms: following a system of daily habits will not only help you achieve quota, it will lead to additional millions in profit for your own pockets, less financial stress, and more mastery of your life. The alternative is to flounder, scrambling at the end of quarters with frenzied work to make up for the lack of consistent daily action. Or, even worse, just crossing your fingers and hoping that some good fortune will bail you out. Please don't choose these alternatives. You'll be miserable and the roller coaster of sales will take its toll on you.

How can you achieve these kinds of life-changing bonuses? Know your numbers, and then break those numbers down to a granular level so you know the tasks you must accomplish each day. Do this, and the world is yours.

KNOW YOUR NUMBERS

If you want to be a sales rep that crushes quota year after year, burn the following three words into your brain: know your numbers.

Let me say that again: KNOW. YOUR. NUMBERS.

There is no way for me to overstate the importance of this. If you don't know your numbers, you will not have a chance at crushing quota year after year. If you do meet quota without knowing your numbers in any given year, consider yourself lucky. And luck is a terrible long-term strategy.

I'm about to go into some detail about what it means to know your numbers and how to break them down. You don't need a PhD in math to grasp this, but it will require you to follow along closely and trust that this will make sense if you follow it through to the end. Once you grasp how powerful this concept is, you're going to be excited about how much more in control you feel when you know exactly what you need to accomplish each day.

Let's dive in and start with the most obvious number of all: your quota. The first thing I want you to do with this number may surprise you, and maybe even scare you a bit. I want you to take your quota number and times it by three. (Eventually, I'm going to suggest you times it by five, but let's start out with three for now.)

Example: your quota for the year is $1 million in sales. That means you're going to change it to $3 million. That's going to be your new target. If you're struggling to meet quota now, that might sound unrealistic but there's definitely a method to this madness.

When you implement the other concepts I'll teach you in this book, what might sound like an extreme goal now will quickly turn into something you can achieve year after year.

But here's the biggest reason to triple your quota goal: if you aim exactly at your quota, there's no margin for error. If you aim at three times your quota and then "only" double your quota, isn't that preferable to barely exceeding quota? So, trust me on this one. Triple your quota. It works. I've seen it happen again and again.

Now that you have a "new" quota, take that number and divide it by twelve months. Continuing with our example, you divide $3 million by twelve and that equals $250,000. Now you know you need to close a quarter million in sales per month (on average).

Next comes the absolutely critical question you need to answer: how many prospective client meetings do you need to have each month to close $250,000 in business? For example, if your average sale is $125,000, and you close on average one out of every three clients you meet with, you need six meetings a month.

(Putting this example another way, if you have six meetings a month, you will likely close two of them. With an average sale of $125,000, closing two sales will put you on target for a $250,000 month. Obviously, you will fill in the appropriate numbers for your own situation.)

Before going on, let's pause for a minute and consider a couple of important things.

First, if you're still a relatively new sales rep just beginning to find your way, you might be thinking, "I don't have enough history to know the number of meetings I'll need, what my close rate will be, or even my average sale." That's a valid objection to bring up, but also one that's easy to solve. You need to talk to your manager and get some guidance. Your manager is likely to be impressed with your initiative and happy to help you figure it out.

The other thing to know is you'll constantly reevaluate all these numbers and make adjustments as you get more data. You're just looking to get started using the best numbers you can, and then keep analyzing and optimizing.

Here are some other numbers that you'll want to take ownership of throughout your career:

- Average number of meetings to get to conversion and to proof of concept (POC), and then from conversion to purchase order.

- Closing rates.

- Average sales cycle.

- Conversion rate from trial to deal.

- The time it takes to complete contracts and/or get an order through procurement.

- Any other impactful numbers specific to your company and sales cycle.

Know the percentages of each of these. Most companies have finance, CRM, and sales operations teams that can assist you with the raw data to figure these out. Use those resources to aid you, but don't settle for information handed to you. Instead, take that data and do your own calculations.

This is all part of the mindset of taking ownership of your career. It's your livelihood and future. Don't cede control of it to anyone else.

Returning to our example, I want you to notice something about breaking down your numbers. Once you figure out the number of meetings you need to triple your quota, you have the key metric you'll need to calculate all your other numbers.

By simplifying things this way, you take the anxiety out of aiming for a huge, abstract number like $3 million in sales for the year. That scary number no longer needs to keep you up at night, wondering how you'll ever hit it. Instead, you become laser-focused on one thing: getting X number of validated meetings a month (and then converting X of these to a POC or trial, and then converting the X number of trials to revenue).

When you concentrate on getting a certain number of validated meetings, suddenly it seems doable. Of course, it will still require hard work, but you'll know exactly what you're working to accomplish.

I should add that I'm slightly simplifying this explanation so you get a quick grasp of what you'll need to crush quota. There will be other dynamics you'll also need to pay attention to, things like how long it takes for a firm to deploy a POC, how long an average sales campaign takes before a prospect says yes to a meeting, how long a company takes to process a purchase order of that size, how long the sales process from an initial meeting to purchase order in hand will take, etc. Don't get overwhelmed with all this right now. Start with the basics and optimize from there.

Now let's return to the process of figuring out your numbers, this time taking it down to an even more granular level. Now that you know how many meetings you need each month, the next thing to think about is what actions will get you those meetings.

Does it take 350 phone calls to get one validated meeting? Does it take 500 emails to get one meeting? Does it take building one relationship with a reseller partner to get a fast-tracked meeting with power? Does it take fourteen various touch points in a campaign (LinkedIn, email, event, call, etc.) to get the meeting?

These are the questions you need to know the answers to better than anyone. It's the foundation of your success, your business, and it will vary for each rep. In time, you'll get a much better understanding of the activity it takes to book meetings, campaigns that will work, events that help, and partners who can aid in speeding up this process.

A quick point I want to make is that the meetings you set must be with properly qualified prospects. Validation can't always be perfect, but if you're just setting meetings with anyone in order to meet a goal, that will backfire.

Assuming you are validating prospects, you'll just need to know how many times you need to repeat each action on average to get a meeting, and then multiply that by the number of meetings you need in a month. This gives you a monthly goal for calls, emails, and other outreach you need to do. (And again, if you need help figuring these numbers out, talk it through with your manager.)

Once you know the quantity of specific actions it takes to get a meeting, it's as simple as dividing those numbers by the working days in the month. Example: let's say it takes 400 calls, 100 emails, and 35 LinkedIn outreaches to land a meeting with a new prospective client. In other words, you don't know which of those will work in any particular circumstance, but you know doing all that combined will likely lead to getting one meeting with a prospective client. If the goal is to get six meetings a month, that means you need to make 2,400 calls, 600 emails, and 200 LinkedIn outreaches every single month (each of those actions times six).

To keep things simple, let's calculate a month as twenty working days. That means you know you need to make 120 calls, thirty email outreaches, and ten LinkedIn outreaches every day. Meet your daily prospecting numbers every day and your pipeline will stay full. And a full pipeline of leads that never goes dry is the secret to crushing quota.

FORMULA RECAP

Quota Given by Employer ($1,000,000) × 3 = Your New Yearly Goal ($3,000,000)

New Yearly Goal ($3,000,000)/12 = New Monthly Revenue Goal ($250,000)

Average Sales Price in This Example = $125,000

Six real meetings needed a month to get two trials installed a month (33% conversion)

Two out of two trials go purchase (100% trial-to-revenue conversion)

- This examples assumes the the trial takes less than a month to prove out and to cut a PO (you'll likely need more time)

- It also assumes a 100% conversion trial to revenue (unlikely; you'll likely need more trial, and more meetings to get those trials)

- The point is to use this example for understanding, and make adjustments to meet more complex realities

From this framework, you can build out what is realistic for each step of your conversion process (outreach to meeting booked, meeting to trial, trial to revenue). You can also build in additional realities not noted above (average sales cycle, etc.) By taking ownership of your numbers, you will have a clear path on where you need to go and what you need to do and book each day to stay on track.

Keep in mind there are other ways to get your six meetings. For example, a more strategic approach could involve hosting a monthly dinner that pulls in six prospects or working with some of your resellers or technology partners to ensure they can get you in front of six folks.

No one way of prospecting is best. The key is that you find a way to do it consistently with real results. Think of the various prospecting methods as tools in your toolkit to leverage for success.

Also, don't be overly influenced by the crowd. Every few years someone will shout, "Cold calling is dead" (most commonly heard from folks who are bad at cold calling). Cold calling and/or warm calling (however you want to spin it) is alive and well, and if done effectively, can help you exceed quota. Over the past decade I've seen thousands of deals start directly from cold calls because they meet a prospect at the right time in their buying journey.

I've also seen many reps take general advice from prospecting products on LinkedIn that share insights like "End your emails with this" or "Say it this way" or "Put this in the header" or "Use this template." This generic insight can be helpful to give you some context, but if copied word for word, it doesn't work. It becomes like a bad cold call—general, robotic, and deleted. Don't follow the crowd and don't fall for the "quick tips to success" advice. Most of your competitors selling on low price are doing just that.

If you're struggling in this arena, seek help from those who cold call/warm call well. Always be aware whether you are cold calling someone's personal cell phone number. Some folks are okay with receiving calls on their personal cell; some aren't. Do your research. If you don't know if it's okay to call someone's personal cell, err on the side of caution.

Whether cold or warm, your goal when prospecting is to be specific and to add value. Do these things and in the end you will triumph. Of course, cold calling is far from the only way to go these days. There are so many great resources and technologies that sales reps can leverage these days. Strategically use them all to achieve your goals.

Whatever types of prospecting you use, do you see the overall beauty of this system? It's a lot like compound interest. The more money you add consistently, the more interest you earn. And then when that interest starts earning interest, you begin seeing exponential results. Time takes care of the rest.

This system of prospecting pays off in a similar way. When you keep adding to your pipeline on a daily basis, you'll be amazed at the flow of leads. Anyone who implements a daily prospecting habit is always astonished at the results. Make sure you focus on tangible outcomes from prospecting instead of simply phoning it in to hit a metric. When you do, your pipeline changes forever. You realize that the whole ends up greater than the sum of its parts. The machine has been created.

Daily prospecting is **the** keystone habit, and without it, you cannot expect to crush quota every year.

Here are the most common questions I get about this system, with answers.

Q: I have more than one number I must meet for my quota. I have to not only hit a total dollar amount in sales, I also have to close a total number of new prospects and sell a certain number of professional services. How will that fit into this system?

A: It's probably much easier to make all your goals fit into this system than you might think at first glance. Typically, if you hit the number of new clients you need, you'll also achieve the total sales and services you need. On a practical level, all you need to do is take each one of your quota goals and break them down. As you go through each one, ask yourself, "If I meet this goal, will I also meet these other two goals?" Once you know the minimum goal you need to meet *all* your numbers, triple it. Then calculate the number of meetings you need to have a month to reach your goal.

Regarding services, run a similar formula. If my goal is $90,000 in services a quarter, then three times will be $270,000. Then I know I need to book on average $90,000 in services a month. On average, you may book two deals per month or need to attach $45,000 in services per order. Then think about things like, how long does the sizing and statement of work (SOW) process take? What products or services engagements lead to higher services closing rates? Can I book more services dollars? These are new numbers you will also need to identify. The key to keep in mind is that you need to figure out what granular actions will help you meet your goal times three.

If two goals require different amounts of meetings, go with whichever number is higher. It gives you the breathing room you need to crush all your numbers.

Q: **What if I don't know how many meetings I'll need to set to close one sale or if I don't know my likely average sale or any other key statistic?**

A: If you're a newer rep, or a rep who is struggling, it's perfectly understandable that you wouldn't have these numbers at your fingertips. But you have to start somewhere, and you need numbers to begin, so...ASK!

You have a manager who can help guide you. There are also likely experienced sales reps who you can talk to about getting a handle on the numbers and how to break them down.

It's also important to add that you should always be analyzing and adjusting these numbers. You're going to get better at all the moving parts that you need to close a sale. For example, if your presentation skills go up and suddenly your average close is one out of every three potential clients instead of one out of four, you can adjust your numbers accordingly.

These improvements should happen over time. When they do, some senior reps fall into the trap of not prospecting as much, letting the better conversion rate make up the difference. This mentality is a trap. You're leaving money on the table and impacting your future quarters. The habit of prospecting is always about consistency. The benefit of higher conversion rates in meeting to trial, trial to revenue, and time of sales cycle are independent of prospecting.

You can use those better conversion rates to multiply your income if you stay consistent with your prospecting. When you drop your prospecting outputs because your conversion rates are better, you're not moving forward and your revenues will stay the same. This mentality of scaling back on hard work will also take a toll on the type of habits you're creating, and the person you're becoming.

Q: **Is it really all about daily numbers or does the quality of my prospecting matter, too?**

A: The quality of your daily prospecting also matters and it's important to remember that the goal is to get *validated* meetings, not prospecting for the sake of hitting a prospecting metric. But it's still your daily number goals that come first. If you're putting in the work every day, and you're still not setting meetings, then something is wrong. It could be your messaging, campaign strategy, ability to overcome objections, outreach times, the contacts you're reaching out to, or something else.

However, too many struggling reps immediately jump to the conclusion that there is a problem with how they're prospecting, when the real problem is they're not doing enough of it.

That said, if you're prospecting hard on a daily basis and don't have meetings to show for it over the course of a month, it's time to make some adjustments. One of the biggest issues I see is not enough follow-up. A big part of your prospecting each day needs to be follow-up; you need to be reaching out to the same prospect in multiple channels, and multiple times in each one. A decade ago, a tech sales rep needed roughly seven follow-ups to get a cold qualified meeting; now I see it takes more than a dozen touches to get the same outcome.

The other big mistake I see is failing to provide unique value when reaching out to prospects. This requires some research instead of just sending an impersonal outreach that boils down to "please meet with me." We'll talk more about this topic in Chapter 6. There is too much noise in the markets for a prospect to respond to just general requests for a meeting. When you do personalized outreach and add value, you rise above the noise.

Another common mistake is not spending enough of your prospecting time trying to connect with partner resellers (also known as system integrators). For companies that work with and through channels, this is an extremely important source for getting client meetings. This topic will be covered extensively in Chapter 5.

There is one other typical pitfall I want to warn you about. When you're a new or struggling rep doing the hard work of prospecting, sometimes getting anybody to respond to you in any way feels like victory.

It's true that a response is better than no response, and there's nothing wrong with feeling positive about it. But it's only relevant if it turns into a meeting. Even a "no" response is good, because it refocuses your energy on prospects who care. But a response never replaces the need for meetings. You can't forget that you must measure daily prospecting success by how many validated meetings you set.

Someone being nice to you is…well, nice. But don't confuse it with setting a real meeting that has the possibility of a revenue generating opportunity. That's the goal of prospecting.

A TECH SALES WARRIOR DAY

What should the day of a quota crusher look like? Probably something like this:

5:45 a.m. to 6:30 a.m.: Your favorite workout to get the blood flowing and then a fifteen-minute meditation or reading to get your mind in the proper place.

7:00 a.m. to 7:30 a.m.: Researching prospective clients.

7:30 a.m. to 9:30 a.m.: Prospecting with your favorite cup of coffee (sending emails, LinkedIn outreach, cold calls).

9:30 a.m. to 11:30 a.m.: Client meetings, internal meetings.

11:30 a.m. to noon: More prospecting.

Noon to 1:30 p.m.: Lunch with a reseller at the hottest restaurant in town. After lunch, make a quick call to the family for a check-in and to send love.

1:30 p.m. to 3:45 p.m: Client meetings, internal meetings.

3:45 p.m. to 4:00 p.m.: Blast your favorite song, get a dance in, or check the news/social media/sports scores.

4:00 p.m. to 6:00 p.m.: More prospecting, breaking it up occasionally with some push-ups or a dance to a favorite song.

Evening: Dinner with a new customer with their favorite chef.

Of course, there will be variations. This is intended to give you an idea of how hard you have to work. I would say if early on you don't have enough client meetings to fill the midmorning and midafternoon time slots, you need to be using that time for more prospecting.

As your pipeline fills up, you can fill those slots and use the early morning and late afternoon for prospecting. But daily prospecting must never fall off your schedule even when you are busy with meetings. If you stop when times are good, you'll create an endless "feast or famine" cycle. That's a recipe for mediocrity. If you follow this process, you'll never miss quota.

NEVER MAKE "AVERAGE" YOUR GOAL

I need to emphasize how important it is to supersize your quota numbers when setting your goals. Don't be intimidated by the idea of tripling them. (And once you master this system, I want you to multiply your quota goals by five.)

I find that average reps always want to seek out average numbers. They want to know what the pack does, and then aim for that. When you aim for average, you're likely to hit it.

Great reps also want to know what the average is. The difference is, they want to know what it is so they can blow those numbers out of the water.

Setting your goals higher will provide cushion in years of economic downturn, when you need time off for family needs, or anything else unexpected. This is when most other reps find themselves missing quota. Higher goals will also take some of the sting out when a deal falls apart through no fault of your own. It happens. Reps with a full pipeline can recover from that; average reps can have their year wrecked by some bad luck.

Is setting your goals at three times quota easy? No. But here's where this book differs from those kinds of self-help books that promise to make everything effortless.

My system is simple, and if you follow it, it will work. But saying it's simple and that it works is not the same thing as saying it's going to be easy.

In fact, the point is almost the opposite: because being a quota-crushing warrior requires hard work, you need a system of daily habits to manage it. As the title of this chapter says, "no one ever met quota in one day." If you don't do the daily work consistently, you're going to need extraordinary luck to exceed quota in any given year.

But as important as the daily grind of prospecting is, it's not all this job is about. The truth is there's a lot of fun to be found in sales, too. So let's lighten things up a bit in the next chapter.

ACTION STEPS FOR CHAPTER 3:

- Take your annual quota and triple it. That's your new goal. (In some cases, you may need to integrate other quota goals into figuring out your "tripled" goal.)

- Next, divide your new goal by twelve. That is the amount of sales you need to do in a month. Figure out how many meetings and trials you need to have with new prospects or customer upsells each month to close that amount of business. That becomes the goal to focus on: how many meetings you need to set a month to triple your quota.

- Figure out the quantity of prospecting actions you need to take each month to hit your meetings goal. Then divide those actions up by the number of days you have in a month to prospect. Those number of actions are your daily prospecting goals (number of phone calls, emails, LinkedIn outreach, events, partner meetings, etc.).

- Make it an ironclad habit to meet your prospecting goal numbers every day. Don't stop when you start seeing success or your pipeline will dry up again. Don't focus on the metric activity of prospecting alone as success; the goal is booking validated meetings daily/weekly to achieve your ultimate goal of closing revenue.

- Adjust and optimize your numbers as needed.

- If you have trouble figuring out these numbers because of a lack of sales experience or you are new to a role, rely on extraordinarily successful reps and/ or your manager to help you set your first goals.

- Know your numbers better than anyone; it's your career. No one will care about your success more than you do.

CHAPTER 4

FINDING THE FUN

---

*"Fun is one of the most important—
and underrated—ingredients in any successful
venture. If you're not having fun, then it's probably
time to call it quits and try something else."*

—Richard Branson

IT'S NOON AND I'VE BARELY MOVED from my chair since 7:30 this
morning. I just wrapped my fifth back-to-back call of the day.

I'm hungry. My eyes are dry from staring into a camera. My brain
is going in too many different directions, and my body feels like it
has weights attached to every limb.

Decision time. I could let that fatigue overtake the rest of my day or…

I can queue the music, crank up the volume, and dance. If I'm really feeling it, I can hit record on my phone, add a goofy Snapchat or Instagram filter (save the TikTok for another day), and share with a colleague who may be feeling lethargic at that very moment, too.

If you're going to be a quota crusher, there's no way to avoid physical tiredness and mental drain. It takes hard work and a burning passion to earn success, and fatigue is an inevitable byproduct of that. But the solution is not to back off the work. Instead, find ways to keep the job fun instead of letting the daily grind chew you up and spit you out.

I call this "Finding the Fun," and it has several aspects to it. First off, it's about finding pockets of fun during your day to let off steam, like me cranking the music and dancing.

Another way to Find the Fun is to remember all the cool things sales allows you to do and to enjoy them. You should also think about all the joy you can bring to clients and colleagues in little but important ways. And one more way to find fun is to turn your mundane daily goals into games where you compete with yourself or accountability partners.

(In Chapter 9, we'll cover deeper and more lasting ways to refresh yourself, including volunteering, daily reflection, and more. This chapter is about finding the little fun things to keep you going; the later chapter will be about the more profound stuff. You need both to keep your sales engine tuned up!)

The first bit of fun we want to talk about are those little pressure release valves you should use every day. Some people think that being fun or even a little silly means you're not serious enough about your work. I disagree. In fact, not only can fun and hard work coexist, they must. If you don't blow off steam, your performance will suffer.

I gave you an example above of cranking up the music and dancing. Here are some more:

- Do a quick set of push-ups.

- Share a video with like-minded colleagues.

- Take a brisk walk outside.

- Grab twenty minutes to dive into a book you're reading.

- Call that friend with the great sense of humor and keep each other laughing.

- Listen to an inspiring podcast or motivational speech.

- If you have young kids and you're working from home that day, get down on the floor and live in their world for fifteen minutes.

These are just examples to get you thinking. The key point is to come up with things that *you* find fun and energizing, without worrying about how others might judge it. It's a proven way to make you more productive, not less.

According to an article in *Fast Company*, methods like Pomodoro, where one works in short bursts followed by short breaks, increase productivity. (Traditionally, the Pomodoro method is twenty-five minutes of work, then a five-minute break, and repeat.) Research from the team at DeskTime found that the top 10 percent of productive people worked an average of fifty-two minutes straight followed by a seventeen-minute break.

I'm not going to try and tell you what's optimal for you. But in tech sales we don't always have the luxury of breaking for seventeen minutes each hour. However, we do have the power to show up with a great attitude and take our breaks for fun where we can find them.

Here's another aspect of Finding the Fun: remind yourself regularly of all the incredible experiences that are built right into your job.

Here are some examples of cool things that are part of sales:

- Taking people out for great meals is a regular part of your job (and it's all paid for!).

- Having the ability to gift prime tickets to a client for a ball game or other cool event (and sometimes going and enjoying it with your client).

- Being the hero by bringing in a delicious, catered spread to an office.

- Traveling to interesting places and meet new people with new challenges, needs, and stories.

- Enjoying a round of golf with beautiful ocean views.

- Attending fun business events like a "casino night."

- Racing Ferraris, Porsches, and Lamborghinis around a track with your customers.

- Going to conferences, learning more, and enjoying all the social time.

- Taking a boat cruise with prospects in Annapolis as the Blue Angels fly over.

- Touring private wine tours in Napa with your strategic integrators.

Maybe not every one of those applies to your particular situation, but I bet you could easily come up with several on your own that do apply.

Reflect on this: how many people would love to have these activities be part of their job description? It's likely a part of yours—how cool is that? Do you remind yourself of it frequently? Do you savor these things in the moment when they're happening?

Enjoy it all. Having this mindset keeps you refreshed and ready to jump back in with renewed vigor for the aspects of the job that are more mundane.

Let's dig just a little deeper into this and think about ways to take joy in making others happy. On a regular basis, you get to take clients, prospects, and resellers out for a good meal at a beautiful restaurant. As an example, it could be a pleasant lunch that follows a morning of prospecting and rejection. You're having lunch in a nice place, in good company, and it's on the expense account. Sure, there's a business purpose to it, but it's a lot more relaxing than cold calls. Are you pausing to enjoy it? And, more importantly, are you taking joy in sharing a meal with someone? This is the mindset that works to keep you from burning out.

(Side note: be sure to consult your expense policy, manager, and marketing team to make sure you are within laws and company policy in advance of dinners/events/gifts to ensure you'll get reimbursed.)

This builds on a vitally important concept that was touched upon in the introduction. It goes to the heart of understanding what sales is (and what it's not).

Looked at in one way, you might be tempted to see your ability to pay for meals and events and gifts in a completely calculated, transactional way. Something like, "I'm doing all this so I get the sale/keep the client/schmooze the reseller." This way of thinking is rooted in the idea of sales as something sleazy, where the best con artist is the best salesperson.

Completely wrong. Don't ever buy into this stereotype about sales. In reality, the most successful salespeople are the opposite of that. The best are the ones that build true relationships and actually care about how they can make a positive impact on the lives of others. They have a deep purpose that comes from having "found their Why" (as we noted in Chapter 1).

If you see your expense account as a kind of a bribe fund, and I can't convince you otherwise, this book won't help you. The "sales-as-manipulation" mentality does not work for the long haul. Occasionally, you'll see someone briefly succeed with it, but it never lasts.

So what's the right mindset? A better way to see it is this: you've been given something special: the ability to make others happy (and enjoy some good times yourself along the way). Recognizing it as a gift that you are blessed to share with others changes everything.

What's the best way to share this gift? The secret is to truly get to know your clients, prospects, and resellers. You listen to them, you find out what gets them amped up, what they do in their spare time, and what is important to them.

This can be as simple as knowing the office you are about to visit has many health-conscious people. Maybe instead of some bakery donuts, you find some high-end juices to bring in to treat everyone.

Or it can be something built on a deeper knowledge of your clients. By forming relationships with them and finding out more of who they are as people, you treat them in a way that makes them happy.

The bonus in all this is that it helps cement your relationship to the client, and that does have a business purpose. But it can't start from a place of manipulation; people sooner or later see through that. It needs to grow out of genuine caring.

To bring this down to the most basic level, Find the Fun by bringing joy to other people. It's another way we're privileged in tech sales. You get to make people happy and often you're along for the ride. Again, how great is that?

There's one more way to Find the Fun that can help push you through those days of daily prospecting and lots of rejection. Turn your daily goals into games.

For example, can you beat yesterday's record for cold calls? Choose whatever metrics you find most challenging and turn it into a game for yourself. Maybe even build a small treat into your day for "winning your game." ("If I do fifteen more LinkedIn outreaches before my 9:30 a.m. meeting, I'll allow myself a dessert at lunch and an extra ten minutes to savor it.")

Another fun thing to do is find a like-minded colleague and compete against each other on whatever metric(s) you choose. It adds an element of both fun competition and friendly accountability.

One last thing. It's easy to think about Finding the Fun, but it's a common failing of many of us to not do it regularly enough. We get caught up in our ambitious work goals. Ambitious goals are fine—in fact they are mandatory for the Tech Sales Warrior. But nonstop work all day long without taking time out for fun will lead to burnout.

Let's pause here for a moment on our journey and look at the groundwork we've laid for supercharging your career. You've found a deep purpose that drives you, and you've found a job that allows you to perform your brand. You know your numbers and have made daily prospecting a habit. And now you know ways to discover some fun so the daily grind won't overpower you.

That's a great foundation, but so far it's been focused mostly on getting YOU ready. But no one can be successful completely alone. It's time to look outward and surround yourself with the right team.

ACTION STEPS FOR CHAPTER 4:

- Think of ways you're going to break up your day with quick exercise, relaxing activities, and sometimes just random fun.

- Reflect with gratitude on all the cool things the job allows and savor those things while they are happening.

- Look for ways to bring joy to others, from the small to the most grand.

- Make games out of your metrics.

- Build the time for these things into your day. It makes a difference in your daily mood and energy!

CHAPTER 5

THERE'S NO "I" IN QUOTA

*"Teamwork is the ability to
work together toward a common vision,
the ability to direct individual accomplishments
toward organizational objectives.
It is the fuel that allows common people
to attain uncommon results."*

—Andrew Carnegie

I WAS ABOUT READY TO GIVE UP ON THE SALE. It hurt to do it, of course, but sometimes you do your best, and it still doesn't happen.

It was December 31, a Saturday, and any deal that wasn't officially closed by midnight wouldn't count toward my sales year. The good news is I was already sitting at more than double my quota. But there was this one more deal sitting out there, and if it fell through, it would negatively impact others on my great team, too.

My manager needed the deal, and my reseller partner sure could have used it, too. For my prospective client, they had to spend these funds or lose them, and the solution I was selling them was something they desperately needed. (And, okay, I wouldn't mind the cherry on top of a successful year!)

If everyone wanted the deal and it was a win all around, why wasn't it happening?

The problem was work schedules near the holiday. There were people on the prospect side who hadn't been in the office between Christmas and New Year's, and there were 'i's to be dotted and 't's to be crossed before the deal could close. All week, my manager and I had been trying to rope this one in, but there was no movement. Finally, the documents got into the hands of the prospect's counsel, but it was Saturday morning and it had to happen that day. The last day of the year.

"There's nothing we can do until we hear back from counsel," the prospect's senior procurement manager told me.

I checked in with the prospect once an hour all morning and there was no news. I called my manager and told him things didn't look good. We both braced for disappointment.

Then things took an even bleaker turn when our partner reseller in the deal texted me. "We're closing down in fifteen minutes for the New Year. It's not coming, right?" I tried the prospect one more time and came up empty again. My manager thanked me for my efforts, and that seemed like that.

With the rest of the day open, I surprised a friend with a last-minute matinee show at the Kennedy Center in Washington, DC. It was the musical with the green witch—you probably know the one. I happen to be a big fan myself. Walking into the swanky lobby wearing a tux, I told my friend, "I don't expect it, but if I get a call during this show I'm going to need to leave. If that happens, you enjoy it, and we'll catch up later for drinks." The show started and it was terrific. I was having a blast. The singing, the stage, and the live music was insanely good!

And then my phone started vibrating. As good as the show was, I wasn't letting this deal go if there was still a chance. Too many people needed it to get done. I waved goodbye to my friend and dashed to the lobby.

"Chris, we have counsel approval, and the purchase order was just cut to your reseller," my client told me. "But we have to be invoiced by tonight. You can make sure that happens, right?"

"I'm on it."

Obviously, I was excited that things were back on. But I also knew this deal would turn into a pumpkin at midnight if it wasn't officially completed by then. And it was 2:30 p.m. on New Year's Eve! But worrying about the obstacles wasn't going to get me anywhere, so I started making calls.

Between my manager and me, we alerted all our teams (finance, legal, sales op, etc.) about the situation. Everyone was on standby, but at the moment we were all blocked from taking action. I couldn't get the partner reseller on the phone to process the purchase order, and nothing could move forward until that happened. I called and texted him literally more than twenty times.

Then I started calling everyone I could think of around him in his company. Still nothing. Finally, in sheer desperation, I called someone who *used to work* for the reseller partner company I needed to reach. He managed to dig up a cell phone number for a manager in the Midwest who might be able to help.

When I reached out to the Midwest manager, he explained he was at a holiday party and the order office was closed.

"I understand, but the client needs it, your rep needs it, and our team needs it. Can someone help us?"

Pause.

"Let me make some calls."

Within fifteen minutes, the rep I couldn't get ahold of earlier called me back. "Dude, my bad. My phone was off and I'm at a holiday party. We're going to get this done."

Over the next four hours, the partner's orders and management teams, along with my company's legal, management, channels, sales operations, and finance teams worked together to process that purchase order.

The client was invoiced at 11:00 p.m. on Saturday, December 31.

To this day, it was one of the sweetest wins in my career. But if you read the story closely, you'll notice that while my persistence was important, it wasn't all about me. There's no way this happens unless several teammates are willing to work together on New Year's Eve to get this deal across the finish line.

This is why the stereotype of an elite salesperson arrogantly making it rain single-handedly is so wrong. The truth is the best salespeople are not lone wolves, out conquering the world by winning business all by themselves. The real story is that top salespeople are the ones who build the best relationships. And that doesn't just mean with your customers or prospects. You have to create excellent relationships within your company and with reseller and technology partners.

Also, never make the mistake of thinking that you should only focus on building relationships with those above you on the hierarchy. Never condescend to anyone and treat everyone with great respect. The people lower in the hierarchy may be putting in sweat equity equal to or greater than your own. And you may need them sometime when you have your own "December 31 at 11:00 p.m." moment. Not to mention, you never know if one of them will become your boss someday!

THE MOST IMPORTANT WORK RELATIONSHIP

Building relationships with your internal team starts with your most important working relationship: your direct manager. Rule number one is to work hard to make yourself a trusted and reliable rep who delivers what's asked.

A sales manager who has your back is invaluable. For starters, this person has at least some say—maybe all the say—in setting your quota.

Your manager can also be there if a deal goes sideways through no fault of your own. Maybe something happens with the partner reseller, or the client, and it's beyond your control. If you've looped in your manager the whole time, and they know you to be someone who is a reliable performer, you have an ally to help protect your reputation within the company.

What are some of the things you can do to build this relationship?

- Be prepared every single time for the weekly forecast call. That means everything is completely up to date and accurate in your CRM. Especially have the proper projected close dates and accurate price quotes in there. Remember that your boss feels pressure, too. Reporting inaccurate or incomplete information up the chain will make your manager look bad.

- Stay in constant communication with your manager. Forget the myth that great salespeople are mavericks out for themselves. The best reps I know are the consistent communicators who never fail to loop their managers in. (And if something starts going wrong with a deal, don't hide it; communicate twice as much!)

- If you're a younger rep, or one who is struggling, ask for advice. Be willing to listen and make changes when your manager recommends it. A good sales manager can end up reminding you of the best coach or teacher you ever had. But you've got to demonstrate a readiness to build that relationship and show them you're receptive to improving.

There's something else that will endear you to your boss more than anything else: consistent performance. Quotas and goals are challenging for sales managers, too. They aren't wild about a rep who crushes it for two quarters and then tanks the next few. Yes, occasionally there can be some misfortune that can cause a blip, but usually inconsistent performance can be directly traced back to a failure to keep the pipeline full.

But that won't happen with you, because you already know how important the daily habit of prospecting is from reading Chapter 3. Nothing bonds you to a sales manager better than being a reliably excellent performer.

Here's a mindset shift that can make a big difference: think of your manager as a business partner. They want to help you succeed, and you want to help them succeed. Ideally, this partnership mentality creates a win for both of you.

A quick note about alternatives if a good relationship with your sales manager is particularly challenging. If you have given an honest effort and your sales manager is providing minimal help and support, try reaching out to the top sales reps in your company. They can be good sources for mentorship when you lack support from your direct report. Use tact and discretion, of course.

After your sales manager, typically the next most important relationship is with your sales engineer.

The specifics of this relationship can vary from company to company, but this is a client-facing person who handles the technical side of installing the software or setting up the hardware. In short, the sales engineer implements the solution you promised the client.

If you're particularly fortunate, you will have a sales engineer assigned all to yourself. But the more likely scenario is a floating sales engineer who works with multiple field reps. Whatever scenario you're in, this is a relationship you want to put effort into. This person needs to know how much you value them.

Have you ever noticed in football that the best quarterbacks often have a tight relationship with their offensive linemen? They give them gifts, compliment them in the media, sometimes cut their own pay so the lineman can be paid more, and they don't throw them under the bus if they have a bad game. The best quarterback understands how key the people in front of him are to his ability to succeed, and he makes sure they know he values them.

Sales engineers need the same from you. They should always understand how much you value them. The sales engineer will be there by your side to answer nitty-gritty technical questions, provide demos, and handle installs. Each of these aspects can make or break your sale.

The most important way to build trust is to always tell the sales engineer what they need to know to be successful with any particular prospect or customer meeting. The key part of that is to make sure the sales engineer is completely looped in on exactly what pain your client wants to solve and the specific goals of a meeting or trial.

Great sales reps identify the business problems being solved and communicate those problems to the sales engineer. In many cases, the solution you're selling has many options and functions. The sales engineer needs to know what this client wants to accomplish and tailor demos and installs to provide that value. The more you can learn to work in tandem with your sales engineer, the more times you'll close a sale successfully.

Your manager and the sales engineer are the two biggest relationships, but you need to treat everyone in your company with respect and build relationships whenever the opportunity arises. There are financial teams, legal teams, sales ops teams, inside sales teams, support teams, overlays, customer success teams, channel teams, and more. Make multiple strong connections in all those departments. Have the attitude that you can't have too many internal company friends, because in tech sales you can't.

I do want to suggest one other internal team relationship that is often overlooked and shouldn't be. That's working with your marketing team on regional events, online marketing, and other creative initiatives. Too often I notice reps who won't even look in this direction. Why would you turn down a potential source of inbound leads to add to the top of your funnel? Explore opportunities with your marketing team and you'll have another way to add to your pipeline.

One last thing about surrounding yourself with a strong internal team: celebrate wins as a team. Spread the credit around because others deserve to hear praise for their contributions and often won't. Always be sincere about it because you can't do this job alone.

In summary, here is what you need to do to be successful with your sales engineer:

- Schedule weekly calls to review upcoming meetings, discuss strategy for upselling existing customers, and determine what specifically needs to be accomplished this week.

- For any existing trial or upcoming trial, isolate what exactly needs to be achieved to meet the business case and ultimately get the PO.

- Get to know your sales engineer outside of work.

- Detail who will cover what points during a presentation with your sales engineer.

- Thank your supporting team members often.

GET THERE FASTER
WITH PARTNER RESELLERS

There's another team you need to have on your side, that's partners or resellers (also known as system integrators). For ease of reference, I'll call them simply "resellers" from here on.

The impact of a good relationship with resellers can't be overstated. Forming strong relationships with resellers is like building a mini army that works with you to accomplish your quota. Imagine having essentially the same quota as in previous years, but now having several people working to help you meet that quota. It's a fantastic situation.

These relationships are so key that I recommend spending about 30 percent to 40 percent of your prospecting time reaching out to resellers when you're in the early stages of building a strong pipeline.

The advantage of resellers is they already have relationships with clients you need to get in front of. One call from a reseller can get you a meeting that otherwise would not happen at all or would require a lot of time-consuming cold prospecting.

This shortening of the sales cycle is invaluable, and the right relationships can change your day-to-day work life and supercharge your career. It will mean less time cold prospecting and more time getting in front of clients.

Another advantage to working with resellers is they typically have access to precious information about their customers. A good reseller can tell you if the prospect has tried other solutions, the likely dollar amount a client will allocate to your product, names of the key decision makers, and more.

In addition, resellers can alert you to internal politics and help you avoid pitfalls that could derail your sale. Finally, they often can help speed up closing the sale by getting the purchase order into your hands faster.

With all these benefits, it's clear that you need to work on partnerships with resellers to get your products in front of prospects. The issue is that you're not the only one who wants to do this, so it can be hard to cultivate the relationship. Where should you start?

Many times, you'll have a channel manager to point you in the right direction. If you're particularly fortunate, they'll walk you right into the door and set you up with a meeting with the reseller.

Industry conferences are another avenue for meeting resellers. Go to the conferences prepared to visit reseller booths. Do a little research on who they partner with and what they do so you have something to reference when you approach them.

When I was starting out, I'd introduce myself something like this: "Hey, I'm Chris. I just started at ABC company. I see you guys resell in the area, and I love what you do with XYZ client. I'd love to share how you can deliver massive value to your customers, make a lot of money reselling my product, and how it could benefit the other products you sell by uniquely doing X." Your objective is to get a meeting with them and take it from there.

Another way to find good resellers is to ask your prospects. Who do they like working with? If they are willing to share that, follow up with questions about why they like working with them, and what the reseller specializes in. If it feels appropriate, ask for an introduction.

If you're a new or struggling tech sales rep, don't go after the "top dogs" right off the bat. Within big reseller companies, there's a hierarchy and you'll be better off aiming to partner with someone there who is as hungry as you are. The top reseller reps don't want to work with diamonds in the rough. Get some polish first.

I remember witnessing two brand-new reps (one at a software company and one at the reseller) working together. They did a classic "one-for-one," meaning "I'll get a meeting, you get a meeting" and then kept rinsing and repeating. They held each other accountable and started to see success. This then morphed into, "I'll get us a deal, you get us a deal."

It was a beautiful partnership because they both worked hard in the trenches together. They closed twelve new customers together in about a year. These guys did not let their inexperience stop them. Find the right partner rep and it will multiply the amount of business you can do. Your success will grow your reputation in the industry and with other partner reps as a natural byproduct.

Also, don't make hard-and-fast judgments based on the size of the reseller company. Some of the biggest reseller players get reputations for being arrogant or being hard to make inroads with. Don't overlook smaller resellers, because many of them have very strong customer relationships. As with any organization, there are no doubt people who are unpleasant to deal with or who don't want to partner with you. Find the people who want to build business together and the ones truly interested in working together. Similarly, don't write off small companies. It's much more about the individuals themselves and the relationship you can build.

Once you find the right resellers to reach out to, how should you start building the relationship? A good place to begin is to think about how the world looks from the reseller perspective.

There's likely anywhere from a dozen to hundreds of other products that share messaging similar to the product you're selling. That means these resellers will have no shortage of other tech salespeople who want to work with them, and there's going to be a lot of noise all around them.

Distinguish yourself from your competition by keeping your messaging extremely concise. Give them two or three sentences about what makes your product unique that they can pass on to clients. In an ideal situation, you're there helping them write emails to clients and at their elbow when pitching to clients. The good ones will appreciate this, because they have so many products to keep track of, they won't necessarily be able to do yours justice without help. You also make a point of knowing what the reseller already sells. Then you can find ways to strengthen and complement their product offerings instead of trying to displace a product that is vital to the reseller's management team.

Here's another way to bond with resellers: come through with a fantastic presentation if the reseller sets you up for a prospect meeting. Prepare like crazy and get whatever help or advice you need from your manager to get the presentation right. The reseller essentially pledged to their customer that meeting with you would be worth their time. Honor that promise by delivering.

A poor meeting and bad response by a reseller's customer is a surefire way to damage a relationship with the reseller. Maintaining a positive customer relationship is paramount to the success of any reseller. As a technology vendor, you need to show up prepared and do exactly what you say you are going to do. Ideally, you wow the customer and make it worth their time.

Finally, when it comes to the terms of the deal, make sure the reseller is making a significant margin. As a general rule of thumb, when the reseller brings you a deal, they would receive a minimum of fifteen points, and it could be upwards of twenty-plus points. If you throw the reseller a deal, ideally you'd give them ten-plus points, which admittedly isn't always possible on tight budgets. (Also, the amount of points can vary by territory and/or with government contracts.)

Remember that you're a rep who is building something, so always err on the side of the smart long-term decision by being generous with points. Plus, it's just the right thing to do to make sure it's a win for everyone. As you progress in your career, you'll also see the value of bringing your strategic partners into a deal early versus only at the end to process paper. The partner will likely be able to add additional values with overall strategy, services, and beyond. As you get pipeline and relationships of your own built, you should reciprocate and bring these resellers into new accounts too.

As time goes by, you'll want to continue to build these reseller relationships. Lunches and dinners and frequent work meetings often morph into attending each other's family functions, cookouts, or attending sports or cultural events together. It's a satisfying part of tech sales that business relationships can sometimes evolve into true friendship. This only happens if you put in the work to build these bonds every week.

Here is a summary of what you need to do to be successful with resellers:

- Always be honest, and always do what you say you're going to do. Consistency is key.

- Reach out to them often. Be persistent without going over the line into obnoxious or annoying. My experience in observing many sales reps is the lack of persistence and follow-up tends to be a bigger problem than obnoxious behaviour.

- Research your reseller to understand how you can positively impact their business with everything else they already sell.

- Never make them look bad in front of the client by being unprepared, running a poor trial, or letting them down. Do what you say you are going to do.

- Find as many ways as possible to make selling your product easy for your resellers.

- When you do close a deal with a reseller's customer, deliver as much value as possible on an ongoing basis. The more you wow this client, the more you make the reseller look good. They won't forget it.

- Share wins with other reps at that reseller to maximize the impact of your deal together and then identify new firms to target.

IF YOU'RE REQUIRED TO WORK WITH A RESELLER, MAKE THE MOST OF IT

You may work for a company that requires ALL transactions be sold through channels, meaning you must always partner with a reseller. This applies even in situations where you did all the work to get the client meeting and essentially sold them without reseller help.

Some sales reps resent this situation. They see it as "I did all this work to drive down the field, and now at the one-yard line I have to hand the ball off and let someone else score the touchdown and take the money from my pockets."

What these reps are seeing as a burden is actually a big opportunity. Let's say you have a three-year deal lined up at $300,000 a year. You go to a reseller and say, "I have a $900,000 sale teed up and I want to give you a 10 percent margin." The resellers get $90,000 without much work at all. Do you think they might remember you? Do you think they'll be more willing to get you in front of some of their other clients? **If the deal comes paired with a services offering, you'll probably have a new best friend.**

Stop seeing working with a reseller as a necessary evil and start looking at it strategically. When you cut a reseller in on a deal that's near the finish line already, choose carefully. For one thing, you need someone you can trust not to mess up your deal. But you also want to choose one that will lead to ongoing partnership that is lucrative for all involved. With some of the bigger resellers, you may need to throw them three or four deals like this before they start paying attention to you, but it will pay off.

You even need to think about looping in resellers even when it's not required of you. (Some tech companies give you the option to do deals without a reseller.) There are times when it will make sense to share some margin by using a reseller when it can lead to even more business later. There's not a one-size-fits-all answer here, but it is something you should consider carefully.

One word of warning: whatever you do, don't ever "pull" or "snake" a deal. Shifting the deal to a different reseller or selling direct after the original reseller helped set things up is an absolute reputation killer. It will not only impact you, but your entire sales team and the overall relationship between the vendor and reseller. Bad business will echo for years. Communication is king, and if a deal is going sideways for any reason, make sure you and your reseller are on the same page for the resolution.

I can't emphasize enough the importance of having a great team around you, both internally and with partner resellers. You can't succeed without investing in these relationships. Always look for ways to expand on these relationships with integration points and by messaging with other leading technology companies the reseller may represent. Remember, make it easy for the reseller and they'll love you.

You have a superb foundation now. You've worked on yourself and you're building a team rooted in strong relationships. But none of it matters if you can't connect with prospects and bring them on as paying customers. The next two chapters will show you how to do that.

ACTION STEPS FOR CHAPTER 5:

- Actively work at building a great relationship with your manager. In particular, commit to making sure your manager never needs to chase you for accurate and timely data.

- Keep your manager in the loop every step of the way of a sale, especially if a problem develops.

- Make sure your sales engineer knows you value him or her. Always set the sales engineer up for success by specifically defining the problem the client wants to solve.

- Be kind and respectful to everyone both above and below you in the company hierarchy. Build relationships in every key department.

- Spend a huge amount of your prospecting time seeking to connect with partner resellers. When you are at the first stages of building a strong lead pipeline, 30 to 40 percent of your prospecting time should be dedicated to this.

- When a reseller trusts you enough to set up a meeting with a client, give it your absolute best effort. Be prepared, on time, and aligned.

- Just like prospecting, building internal and external relationships takes daily effort and is a lifelong journey. Make it a part of what you do every day and the benefits will come.

CHAPTER 6

YOU CAN'T SELL THEM UNLESS YOU KNOW THEM

"People don't care how much you know until
they know how much you care."

—Theodore Roosevelt

THE REP HAD JUST BEGUN leading her own meetings. This was her breakout moment after her initial training when someone else ran her meetings. Now she would be the one in command.

She researched the client, she got to the meeting ten minutes before it started, she was prepped to win, and then proceeded to talk all the way through a thirty-minute discovery meeting. With three minutes to spare, she got around to asking a question of her prospect: "How does that sound to you?"

Answer: "It's not really relevant to us."

OUCH.

This rep worked hard to get the meeting, she was smart and competent, but she fell for the fatal flaw of making the meeting about her company and her product instead of her prospect's pain and needs. Making this experience even worse, the rep *did* have a solution that would've worked beautifully. But by then it was too late because she'd already shredded her credibility with the prospective client with a thirty-minute monologue of marketing.

It's easy to shake your head at the rep's obvious mistake in this story, but the truth is many reps make similar errors all the time, it's just not always quite as glaring.

I've also often witnessed reps asking great questions, receiving responses that are absolute gold, but then failing to use those answers to relate back to the product or service they're selling.

Other times, reps fail to see that the answers they are getting disqualify the prospect, and they go on to waste lots of time trying to sell a company that is not the right fit.

The root of these kinds of mistakes is a fundamental misunderstanding of your job. **You are not pitching a product. You are providing a solution to a problem.**

To sell a solution, it must match or exceed what's needed to solve your prospect's problem. Priority number one is a deep understanding of the pain your prospect is experiencing because they lack a solution. And the only way to uncover that is to ask a lot of questions.

As we dive into this topic, you need to keep one bedrock principle front and center at all times: it's not about you. It's not about your product. It's about your prospect's and customer's pain, and specifically how you can make their businesses and their lives better.

Getting to know your future customer starts during prospecting. For example, let's say you're sending a cold email. Do a quick bit of research so you can provide some value in that email. Share a relevant article through email, comment on a company LinkedIn post, reference a recent talk the prospect gave, or congratulate the company on a recent accomplishment. Way too many reps send cold emails that are nothing more than a plea to have a meeting. They also fail to use the information the prospect shares with them, which may be vital to their needs and a great way to build authentic rapport.

Outreach with a little research has a much better chance of success, but it has another benefit, too. It lays the groundwork for knowing your client if you do score a meeting with them. In the past year, I've received hundreds of emails and calls from sales reps selling a general solution to boost sales productivity, and only one made the effort to personalize their outreach. And zero followed up with enough value or enough times to make a meeting a must. Imagine how your own prospecting will stand out if you add unique value with each outreach and continue to follow up.

Once you do get a response from a prospect, you need to validate that they have a problem you can solve. Ideally, you'll be validating that the prospect is a match with each successive follow-up. You don't want to waste time going to meetings with prospects that don't have a problem big enough to warrant paying for your solution. If you find yourself at meetings where there is no alignment between problem and solution, you're not doing enough validation before setting meetings. If this becomes a consistent problem, reach out to your manager, education team, or top consistent sales reps at your company to figure out what you're doing wrong in the qualification process.

But let's say you have validated appropriately, and now you've successfully set up an initial discovery meeting with a prospect. It's time to dig even deeper into this concept of knowing who they are.

First off, a professional prepares for a meeting. And I don't just mean practicing your presentation (although you better do that, and often!). Preparation means gathering basic information about the company, knowing the room you are walking into, and what the goal of the meeting is for them and for you. Many times, reps will go into a meeting and they don't even know what the client does. It's shocking to me, but they will literally walk in without knowing what the client specializes in, what their product is, how they make money, recent news in the media, and other easily found information.

Reps who don't do this up-front work think they are just selling their product to whomever wants to buy it, when what they need to understand is that they're selling a solution to a specific company that has a specific need and pain. Poor preparation is what gives sales the bad rap it can sometimes have. It also marks the unprepared rep as an amateur. Don't be an amateur.

By the way, for this initial meeting, I'm not suggesting you need to spend hours and hours researching. Thirty minutes of research is usually plenty. Make a few notes for yourself and that's enough.

Here are some good things to look for when researching a potential client:

- If it's a public company, find and read its 10-K (every public company is required to file one with the SEC).

- Search the internet and the *Wall Street Journal* online for any mention of the company in the news.

- Check out LinkedIn for things like company size and whether they have any content posted there. You can also look there for clues to see if they're a growing company.

- Work with your resellers or other technology partners to share information about the company.

- Explore whether you have any common connections on social media.

- Other potentially useful information sources are Google searches for news alerts about the company, and the company's own website and blog. (The website will often have the annual report posted somewhere; you should read that, too.)

- Use the information you learn to stand out from the noise. Too many reps go into a meeting without specific information and try to rely on buzzword name drops ("We help with ransomware, encryption, DDOS, backup, etc."). Guess what? Every one of your competitors is using those same buzzwords. That's just a crutch. Talk about their specific problems and how your firm can uniquely solve those issues.

I should also mention that some tech sales companies subscribe to extraordinary marketing tools that are truly awesome for this kind of research—another reason to befriend the marketing department. With a few keystrokes, you can get detailed information about your prospect, including what they're searching for online, what they've been purchasing, what they're worried about, accurate contact info, and the company's strategic initiatives. There are now dozens of amazing sales and marketing tools out there.

It's stunning to me that some sales reps have this goldmine at their fingertips and don't use it. And they don't spend any time in their off hours understanding how they can make the most of this technology. If your company provides tools like this (which often cost thousands or even millions of dollars), use them. Some of the competitors you're up against would love to have the same capability. And great sales reps of the past could only dream of having these kinds of tools.

After gathering company info, next drill down to who specifically you'll be meeting with. You'll want names and titles at an absolute minimum. If you're working with a reseller or another technology partner who works with the prospect, they can tell you much more, including how long someone has been there, where each person fits into the hierarchy of the organization, what their duties are, relationship dynamics, business challenges, personal likes/dislikes, and other practical information.

Even if you don't have a reseller or technology partner who can provide all these details, you can probably figure at least some of this out with some savvy Google and LinkedIn searches.

The final piece to meeting prep is to understand as clearly as possible what they want to accomplish during the meeting. Sometimes this will emerge out of your initial prospecting and follow-up. This is also an area where a reseller can be a great help. However you get the information, the more you can understand about what the client wants out of the meeting, the better it will go. You may also need to request additional people from your company to join you to make the most of the meeting. Knowing that ahead of time shows the power of prep work.

RECOMMENDED RESOURCES FOR IMPROVING YOUR SKILLS

Here's a list of proven sales methodologies. Research them online and read books that detail these methods and adopt what's useful.

- BANT (Budget, Authority, Need, Timeline)

- Value Selling

- Sandler

- The Challenger Sales Method

- MEDDIC

- SPIN

- Gap Selling

And here are some books to review on negotiation and sales:

- *Never Split the Difference* by Chris Voss

- *Predictable Revenue* by Aaron Ross and Marylou Tyler

- *Influence* by Robert B. Cialdini

- *The Perfect Close* by James Muir

- *Getting to Yes* by Roger Fisher, William L. Ury, and Bruce Patton

- *Sales Differentiation* by Lee B. Salz

- *Inked* by Jeb Blount

If your goal is to be a mega successful sales rep, I want to give you a bonus piece of advice. At the minimum, the most successful reps keep a notebook on every client all the way through the process, from prospecting, to initial research, on through meetings, closing, and postsale client relations. The more advanced reps will keep track of personal likes, birthdays, favorite sports teams, interests, favorite restaurants, and more.

It's like their own personal set of data points about all their business relationships. Sometimes when someone changes companies, the rep will cross paths with one of the folks he took notes about a few years back. Now the rep has that background to build on. If you want to play at the highest level, this is how the best reps do it. There are many software products out there to help you keep track of this data over time if you desire to transfer from journal to screen. (Obviously, you'll want to make sure it's protected from cyberattacks, and within company policy.) Now that you've done all the prep, it's time for the meeting. And I want you to go into this meeting using a combination of three alter egos or mindsets: you're a blank canvas, you're a detective, and you're a doctor. Leveraging these personas will help you focus on what you're there to do.

Relying on these personas can help you overcome the fear of presenting to a roomful of C-level executives. By putting on these personas, you can separate yourself from your anxieties and perform your role. For more about this concept, I recommend reading a superb book, *Alter Ego* by Todd Herman.

Let's now take each of these mindsets—blank canvas, detective, and doctor—in turn. You want to approach the meeting as a blank canvas, which means you don't want to go into the meeting with preconceived ideas that you already know all about the client's problem.

That might at first seem to contradict what I said above about doing research and validating the problem before you set a meeting. Having that background will be invaluable, but you don't want to lock yourself into a narrative about what this client needs before meeting with them. Come to the meeting with fresh eyes or you could miss important data points.

These are called "discovery" meetings for a reason. You're there to discover as much as you can about the client. You want to know the major players, how urgent their problem is, why it's important now, the personal and business pain, and what exactly they need to see to prove success to move forward with a purchase.

In all this, preconceived ideas are the enemy, and that's why you need to be a blank canvas. That's also the perfect lead-in to the next mindset you'll need: detective.

During the meeting, you'll need to be the analytical detective, and the case you need to crack is the client's basic business problem. You're also seeking clues to who the key players are and who holds the authority to make a decision.

Related to this, pick up on signals about who cares about this in the company. Is this being driven from the C-level executive suite? If it's not and you're selling a six- or seven-figure solution, you'll likely have very little chance of closing a deal.

You're also seeking to uncover the client's budget for this project. You want to talk about money early in the sales process, and you want to talk about it often. The exact timing of when to bring it up is a skill you'll need to develop. You might need to bring it up in the first meeting, or maybe it will be the fourth meeting. What's important is to read the room and understand the prospect's need and timing for your solution. This will be covered in more detail in the next chapter, but for now just understand that you want to talk about budget range as soon as possible.

That's the detective work you'll be doing throughout the meeting. But you'll need one more persona: doctor. Probe for the pain. Where does this problem hurt their bottom line? How much does it hurt? How long has it been painful? Is there any immediate reason why they have to change today, and if so, why? You don't want to rush through this process. Explore what their lack of solution is costing them and look at what pain there will be in the future if they don't solve it.

A good doctor doesn't stop on the surface. Doctors keep the questions coming until they can nail down the precise source of the pain. And the best doctors let their patients tell them where the pain is. You need to do likewise.

The doctor's questions drive toward three purposes:

- You're reminding the client of their pain, how much it is costing them, and how much it will cost them in the future. This makes them more readily see the value in finding a solution sooner rather than later. When done with the utmost skill, your questions will actually lead the prospect to share how their problems will best be solved by implementing your solution due to X impending event. A good thing to remind yourself: don't force it, just ask better questions.

- You're finding out how their problem and pain maps to your products and solutions. Remember, it's not about your product, it's about how it solves their problem. Exploring your prospect's true pain (business and personal) will show you where to put your emphasis as you explain your product.

- As you keep asking questions about the pain and going to deeper levels, you may see things that the prospect or customer doesn't see about how much this problem is costing them. You can then educate them on those costs, further adding value to your relationship with them. (More on this in Chapter 7.)

There's something else that a young or struggling rep needs to learn about these initial meetings, and that's when to keep pushing and when to stop. This is one of the nuances of complex B2B tech sales. They're called complex because no one is going in and closing on a solution that costs $100,000+ a year in one step. You're steadily building toward a sale. You want each meeting to be another step forward, and that involves knowing when to keep talking and when to slow it down.

This is where you need to remember that you're there to serve your prospect's or customer's best interests. This service mindset means you're looking for ways to match the solution to their problem in a time frame that makes sense for their business (and yours). Of course, if the solution you're providing is truly urgent, then it's also up to you to do your best to educate your client on that fact and accelerate the deal based on those needs.

It's also worth noting that sometimes there are obstacles beyond your control. Some companies will need you to sign a nondisclosure agreement (NDA) before discussing details of their business with you. If that's not in place by the first meeting, the client will want to focus on hearing about your product first, and diving into deeper discovery once an NDA is signed. Not ideal, but top reps adjust and work within the context of the situation. For these meetings, you'll likely want to cite real-world business case studies or recent problems solved with other unnamed companies so that the problem/solution becomes something real to your prospect (instead of a product just being sold).

As you go through successive meetings, you'll become less of a blank canvas and your role will become more of a thought leader on how to solve the problem. But many of the underlying ideas will remain the same in subsequent meetings. You'll continue to seek ways to understand the different facets of the client's problem and the pain it causes, and how to align it with your solution. You should do detailed follow-up to show them how exactly you are achieving those outcomes to transform their current state of operation.

It's important throughout this process that you and your sales engineer are documenting the success criteria, continuously sharing what has been achieved so far and what's coming next. If you reach the trial stage, keep detailing what needs done to move forward with a purchase and make sure the timing is understood and agreed to by all parties.

Don't forget that you must always make sure the C-level executives stay in the loop. It's not enough to make sure all this is happening; you need to also make sure that the power at these companies know it's happening and are on board with the process.

SPECIFIC MEETING STRATEGIES
OF TECH SALES WARRIORS

Here are specific strategies and tips that can be useful in any client-facing meeting:

- Keep marketing fluff about your company to a minimum. No one wants to hear a long-winded company history or generic statements about how wonderful your products are. (When introducing your company, allocate fifteen seconds to one minute to establish credibility.)

- Recap what the focus of the meeting is as far as you understand. Ensure your prospect or customer is on the same page, and ask if you are missing anything. If they add to the agenda, verbally restate what it is they said so you are both on the same page. They will appreciate your listening skills.

- Transition out of any introductory statements in less than a minute. Next, make sure that the expectations for the meeting are aligned. "To be respectful of your time, I just want to confirm we have sixty minutes together today, is that right?" Also ask if anyone has to leave early. If the most important person to your deal has to leave in twenty minutes, cover the most crucial topics in the first twenty minutes.

- Have your notebook out in every meeting and furiously take notes. I recommend a notebook over typing notes on a laptop or device, which can make you look unengaged with your head buried in a screen.

- One crucial purpose of note-taking is to remember who has what concern and where they sit in priority for this project to be approved for purchase. You should ask things like, "John, if I heard you right, your main concern is X. Do I have that right?" and "Mary, you said any solution would have to accomplish Y. Is that correct?" And so on. Ask them to prioritize the importance of all this for their company and for the project at hand. It's impressive to the clients and lets them know you've truly been listening.

- Here are two golden questions that should be used in every single meeting, multiple times: "Is there anything else about X I should know?" and "Did I miss anything about what's most important to you?" Give them open-ended questions and then listen. If your prospects keep sharing about the project at hand, keep your ears open and your hand busy writing.

- Always work to quantify the problem. How much is it costing them in real dollars and over how long a period? Why do they need to solve this today? Always bring things back to the cost of inaction. This is a business decision after all, so you need to put it in the language of business: money. Leveraging their own deadlines can help you work a deal using a reverse timeline. "If you need to have this solution in place by July and procurement takes a month in June, we would need to wrap the trial by the end of May. This likely means we would need to be installed by April 15. Does that time frame make sense to you?"

- Keep in mind that a sale is never exclusively about numbers. You want to understand the human problem. What will it look like if they don't solve this? How often are they hearing about this problem? How much pressure do they feel about it? In some cases, the lack of a solution has deeply personal consequences for a person's job, career, and home life. Ask them questions and let them tell the story of what doing nothing looks like.

- An overall recap at the end of each meeting and setting of next steps is a best practice. This is particularly important if multiple teams have been involved in the meeting.

I also want to recap three goals you should have for every client meeting:

- That you constantly validate the alignment between your solution and the client's problem (including budget alignment).

- That you understand who holds the decision-making power for your deal and how invested they are in finding a solution.

- That progress is made each meeting, with a clear next step (including a date and time) to move things forward.

This last point is particularly important. A deal can take a small handful of meetings, or it can take 100+ meetings. There's no single right answer to how many are needed. But if the number of meetings keeps growing, you need to check yourself by asking at the end of each one, "Do we have a clear next step and date/time associated to achieve this outcome?" Ask yourself, "Am I arbitrarily coming up with these dates/times or does my prospect/customer have the same vision?"

You don't need to make huge leaps every meeting. As long as you are progressing in achieving the original success criteria laid out and have a clear next step, you're on the path toward closing.

Speaking of closing, it's time to find out the best ways to get your deals across the finish line.

ACTION STEPS FOR CHAPTER 6:

- Never forget that you aren't pitching a product; you're providing a solution.

- Prepare for engaging with clients by doing research during prospecting and before the initial discovery meetings. Know the people attending and the goal of the meeting.

- Ask a lot of questions during meetings and marry the responses to your solution constantly.

- Ask great questions to lead your prospects and customers to think about the cost of doing nothing or going too cheap.

- Make sure every meeting ends with a recap of what was accomplished and a clear next step with date and time.

CHAPTER 7

CLOSING THE SALE

"If a deal is ready, close it.
This eliminates such risks as the buyer leaving
his job or the market tanking."

—From the Rudnitsky Sales Playbook quoted in
Behind the Cloud by Marc Benioff and Carlye Adler

NEGOTIATION IN LARGE TECHNOLOGY transactions can often be
complex, long, and tedious. In some cases, by the end, both parties
are worn out and just want it to be over.

It doesn't have to be that way.

I'll never forget a deal that started at happy hour at a crab shack in
Baltimore and ended a few short weeks later with smiles all around.

The happy hour was sponsored by a reseller I worked with. It was a beautiful evening, with amazing food and excellent music, all of it on the waterfront.

The atmosphere had me in a great mood when I saw someone off by himself taking in the sunset. I asked my reseller if that was her customer.

"Yes, it is. That's John. He's the CIO of a local county government."

"Oh wow, he'd be good for me to meet. Do you mind if I go introduce myself?" I asked.

The reseller was all for it, and I walked over to him. He was enjoying a beer and seemed to be in his own space. I wasn't sure I should interrupt him, but I decided to take a risk. After all, opportunities are precious.

"Hi John, I'm Chris with XYZ company. I work with Lauren with a bunch of other counties and universities. Are you familiar with XYZ company?"

"No, I'm not."

"I know this is odd at a happy hour, but do you mind if I give you a quick pitch on how we help other counties like yours and see if it's relevant for yours?" I asked.

"Shoot."

I pitched for thirty seconds and checked in to see if this was relevant to John. It was.

John and I discussed how we could help him with an immediate need in a situation where he hadn't been able to find another solution. He did most of the talking. I listened. He asked for rough numbers and I gave him the range.

A week later, John pulled my team in for an onsite demonstration with his entire team. Within another week, we had installed our product. During the install time frame, our company gave extra effort by fighting off an active cyberattack, which wasn't part of their ask for the project to be considered a success. We provided the value anyway.

A month later we had a purchase order in hand for $500,000+, and this client continued to buy products from us for years after. The entire deal felt like a win-win all the way through. No losers, just partners from day one. The rough price range I gave him on the fly at happy hour never changed (which is why it pays to know accurate rough numbers for your product or service off the top of your head, or at least a range).

John no longer works for that county and I no longer work for that team, but it was such a win-win that we still check in with each from time to time. We grab lunch when we find ourselves in the same city.

This is how negotiations and closing can go when you treat your customers like partners instead of just another transaction. Match the client's need with the value you can provide. Align it with the budget range and make sure your team executes during the trial on the value you promised. Do what you say you are going to do and hold each other accountable to the timelines laid out from the beginning. Your chances for an efficient close go way up when all this happens.

Will it always go as smoothly as the transaction that started at a crab shack happy hour? No. That was a particularly ideal example. However, I do promise you that the more you work on the front end to align client problems and needs with the value of your solution, the more deals you'll close with relative ease. You'll also want to make sure there's a budget match early in the process (which may happen at meeting one or meeting three, but definitely well in advance of any wrap-up), and that your team performs during the trial as you outlined from the beginning.

This is why the previous chapter about knowing your client could've been called "Closing the Sale, Part One." Everything you do to further your knowledge of a client and the problem they want to solve is laying the groundwork for the close. Done right, it should be one seamless process where you're not sure where discovery ends and closing begins. It's all about constantly looking for alignment, documenting as you go, and following through.

If you recall from the previous chapter, we touched upon aligning budget with the costs of the solution. The advice was to talk about money early and often. Let's get even more specific and detailed now.

Many struggling reps are afraid to bring up budget. That's a big mistake and in some cases can impact negotiations. The fear of dialogue about pricing and budgets reveals itself in different ways, but it all leads to the same problem: not getting aligned with the client's budget early enough in the process. It's often driven by not understanding that what you are selling will transform their business. It's why many deals don't end up happening and causes huge amounts of wasted time on all sides.

If you're doing any of the following, it's a sure sign you're struggling with this issue:

- Not bringing up price until the very end of the sales process (right about the time you're ready to ask for a PO).

- During client presentations, you delay talking about rough costs as long as possible even when the CIO from the prospect has requested for a rough range three times in a row and has provided you with all the details you need to build a range.

- When you share pricing, you're borderline apologetic about it.

- Getting nervous when the prospective client asks any question related to pricing. This jumpiness about price causes you to start giving them lower cost options they didn't ask about.

- You don't come across as confident or at ease when you are reviewing the budget range with your prospect.

- The majority of your trials or POCs stall at the end or somehow always seem to magically disappear.

If any of the above sound familiar to you, it's crucial that you figure out why and then get it fixed. In my experience, the struggle of talking about price is rooted in three things.

For one, we all have a way of relating to money and making purchasing decisions that is based on our life experiences (often going back to our childhood and how our family taught us to relate to money or how you purchase large items yourself). You carry those ideas into how you sell, often without even realizing it.

The second issue is also related to mindset. Are you approaching the sale with the confident knowledge that you're truly solving a significant problem for your client? That's the right mindset. But too often, sales reps are stuck in a mentality that sales is about convincing people to buy something they don't need. This myth can subtly work against you and make you feel less confident about the price of your product.

The third is about your skills as a presenter. Do you understand how you come across in your pitch, your tone and style? Is your messaging clear and to the point or is it all over the place? Do you seem natural and human, or forced and robotic? Are you apologizing for your pricing? Do some introspection about the current level of your presentation skills. This is an area where seeking out a coach or mentor can be especially helpful.

If those are the most typical problems, how can you work through them and get better at addressing price-budget alignment early and often?

Here are three suggestions:

- To help solve the problem of bringing your own assumptions about money into the process, do some journaling. Work through how you make your own large buying decisions and the assumptions behind those decisions. Relate that to how it may be negatively impacting your interactions with clients. Often when we examine our own assumptions, we find they don't hold up to scrutiny and that prompts positive change.

- Similarly, you need to examine why you're not more confident in the value of the product you're selling. The whole idea of selling is to genuinely care about making your prospects' and customers' lives better by solving significant issues for them. You're delivering something of substantial value to them and it will cost them less than failing to address the problem.

- I recommend reading your company's own internal customer case studies, ROI studies, and customer testimonials to understand the impact your firm makes in people's lives. When you see these firsthand, it will empower you to be more confident in your prices and products.

- The final suggestion is to get help from your sales manager as you learn the art of aligning product cost with client budget. Rely on that expertise and learn from it. Sales managers can help you customize pricing conversations and proposals for specific clients. The best ones will even run boot camps or role-plays on this topic so you can get better in a safe space. You can also seek a coach or mentor if your manager or education team doesn't offer this. This can be invaluable for reps learning to get a handle on talking price and make you more confident in your conversations and presentations.

It's important to remind yourself why bringing price into the conversation early and often is so important to the health of your deal. If your prospect has a $100,000 problem, and you're selling a million-dollar solution, that has zero chance of ending well.

But if the prospect has a million-dollar problem and your solution is $250,000, you may be in alignment. Even better when you find a problem that's five times or more the cost of your solution. Then the question is simply this: "John, this could cost roughly $350,000–$500,000 per year based on the project goals and timing. Does this look doable?" Once you get the affirmative, you've made the first step towards locking in a range and working towards the final pricing of the solution.

There will be other times when the client doesn't understand how much their problem is costing them. It's your job to show them with facts and data. Then negotiation becomes education instead of dropping your price to reach alignment.

Dropping the price is not always an option, but even when it is, the belief that negotiation is all about slashing the price is false. You may be jumping to the conclusion that the problem is price when it's not. And if the price is identified as a problem, you need to know your limits and how low you can go before you need to walk away from the opportunity altogether. Working closely with your deal desk and manager, you will eventually know those limits.

Remember, sometimes saying yes on some little things is a way to hold the line on bigger things, like price.

There's not a one-size-fits-all solution when budget alignment is in the ballpark but you're not all the way there yet. The best approach is to continue to dig deep into the client's pain and how your solution addresses that pain. Who at the company needs this solved? What's on the line for them (both personally and for the company)? The more you understand, the more you can find a way to alignment.

I need to throw an important disclaimer in here when it comes to talking about price early and often. Don't confuse this with a situation where a prospect asks for pricing without sharing what their project goals and specifications are, and you are just sending over a blind quote or number. Avoid that.

Similarly, don't send a quote over to a company or individual who has no say in the purchase process. And don't give in to a project manager pushing you for pricing when you don't have a clue what they actually need yet. Talking about price early and often does not mean throwing random darts. That will only put your company in a bad position later to even make an attempt to execute on a very low price.

Pricing is another perfect opportunity to rely on the relationship with your sales manager or a successful rep mentor and get your sale across the finish line.

Before presenting pricing, talk through it with your manager. He or she may have great insights into overall strategy, what has worked in the past, and landmines to avoid. Review how other sales leaders in your firm have positioned pricing in the past to make it a win for your prospect as well as for your company.

Avoid the notion that success in a negotiation is always about dropping a price. Dropping a price too far and too often eventually destroys margins, lowers perceived value, and negatively impacts your company's price book, which eventually leads to impact on revenues and your standing in the marketplace.

Another thing that was mentioned briefly in the last chapter was locating the power sources for this deal. This becomes absolutely crucial for getting the deal closed. Find out who cares about the issue you're solving inside the client's company. Discover who holds the purse strings and the final decision-making power. This may be one person, but the larger your deal gets, the more likely it is that several people will have to sign on to get it across the finish line.

In short, you need to align with power as early as possible, too. You can end up wasting a lot of time if you don't nail down early in the conversation who has the power and how much this matters to them. Again, you do this by asking a lot of questions. Yes, you need to be tactful about it, and you certainly don't want to be dismissive of anyone during the process, but you do need to get in front of the decision makers as soon as you can.

You can also blow a sale by talking too much. It's a common mistake of struggling reps.

For example, a client asks a simple question: "What is the contract length?" It deserves a simple answer, like "It's a five-year term." But some reps will immediately say, "It's a five-year term, but we could do a three-year term, or possibly a two-year term. In fact, maybe if you really want it, we could do a one-year term."

What is that? Why all the options before they even objected to the answer? Give simple, direct answers to questions. Choice overload confuses prospective buyers and can kill a deal.

Here's the other reason talking too much is a bad idea. It stops you from listening. Often when you're talking, you're wasting the prospect's time with things they may not even care about, or worse, talking yourself out of a deal. That's time you should be spending asking good questions and listening to the prospect talk, and then leveraging those responses to move the deal forward.

If you continue to struggle with negotiation, I again recommend the Todd Herman book *Alter Ego*. Negotiation is an absolutely critical skill, and the book highlights how elite sport players and business professionals use "alter egos" to get over their fears and still perform in the moment. You can use this concept to separate yourself from your anxieties about tough questions and big numbers, and still execute when the pressure is on.

Prospect personality can affect how you close as well. During discovery, you should be noting your prospect's decision-making style. Are they a no-nonsense, "just the facts" kind of person? Or do they seem to make decisions based on some broad understanding married with a gut feeling? Or maybe they're a personality that likes lots of reassurance.

One of the most fun and challenging parts of sales is discovering people's personalities, including how they buy, and then adapting your delivery of information based on that knowledge.

DETAILS MATTER

Let's say you get a verbal commitment, or even better, a written commitment via email that the deal is a go. You're not nearly done. Until the purchase order lands at your company anything could happen.

Where do you begin? First, be extremely detail oriented about the quote. The beginner's mistake is to rush a quote and immediately send it over to a client.

No, never do that. Double-check your work. Then triple-check it. Then get another set of experienced eyes on it (likely your sales manager's). Do the same if you sell through a reseller.

Always check the details, including SKUs, descriptions, line items, length, cost, etc., and do it before it lands with the client. You also should schedule a call or in-person meeting to review the quote and answer any questions about it. If you launch a quote over the fence without scheduling a call, you lose all power in the selling process. During a quote review, it's important to get feedback, field any objections, and look for any red flags that may derail your sale.

Another common mistake many young reps make is limiting the scope of software or services in the quote to meet a price point versus finding a different price point that could be negotiated to make the prospect happy. If you short the quote, the prospect's objectives won't be met. It lowers the price, but it will be a nightmare for everyone postsale because the build won't solve the problem discussed at the start. The quote must cover adequate resources for the client to be satisfied. Make sure you are up front about this throughout the negotiation process.

With each quote you work on, you'll keep improving your quoting skills until they are super strong (which is a hugely valuable skill in tech sales). You'll also find ways to provide more value to your clients and get more efficient at putting quotes together. Like the prospecting skills you learned about earlier, good quoting skills will stay with you for your entire career.

Good quotes also set up the rest of your company's team for success. A clearly defined scope of work and an adequate product scope leads to a seamless, client-centered, "wow" type of experience—not just for your prospect, but also for your reseller, your sales-ops team, your finance team, and your legal team. In quoting, there are a lot of people counting on you to nail the details. Get them right the first time.

Not only do you want to be detailed, you also want to be as fast as possible in getting the closing completed once you have a commitment. Unexpected things can happen that can kill a deal you thought was in the bag. The old saying "Time kills all deals" is true. People change jobs, another department may steal budget, a company gets acquired or divested or merged, a new CFO wants to weigh in on a decision, or priorities may change at the last minute. In other words, anything can happen, so move efficiently. Until the purchase order is in your hands and your company has invoiced, there is risk.

Also remember that you'll close more sales with a can-do attitude. Your focus should not be on negativity or trivial things, and don't get caught up in battles between departments. Not everything will be in your direct control of course, but be a problem solver whenever you can. Find the path to the PO. Once you have an overall general agreement with a prospect or customer, your attitude should always be that you'll do what it takes to get a finalized purchase order in hand.

One final piece of advice: once you finally sign on a customer, the work is far from over. Start obsessing about your customer's one-, three-, and five-year goals. Establish quarterly meetings to highlight ROI. Understand the strategic vision of the company's board and find ways that your solutions can help achieve it.

You not only want to keep the business, you want to find ways to upsell your customers that is a win for both of you.

ACTION STEPS FOR CHAPTER 7:

- Talk about budget alignment early and often.

- Find out who the power is on the client side and align with that power as soon as possible. If it's multiple people, make sure you connect with each.

- Triangulate the information you know and continue to validate with the prospect throughout the sales process.

- Clearly differentiate to set your solution/service apart from the buzzword noise (i.e. "We help with ransomware.") What specifically will your solution do? How is it unique?

- Set your future customer, your reseller, and your own team up for success by quoting the proper scope of the project. Always triple-check that you have the quote right before it lands with the prospect. If you send quotes through a reseller, you should be double-checking that their quote to the customer is accurate, too.

- Work with your manager and other sales leaders to perfect your "go to market" selling strategy for at least your first six deals. Never be afraid to have another leader review your pricing strategy, pitch, and quotes throughout your career.

- Use a reverse timeline to establish clear deadlines leading up to the purchase.

- Be thorough and document the process in detail to keep everyone on the same page.

- Review quotes in person or on a call to get feedback and address any concerns live.

- Be a problem solver. Bumps will happen, but it's all worth it when you have a happy customer and a completed sale.

- Once a deal closes, never think that means the work is over. Not even close. Ensure your customer is getting value quickly. Avoid being focused on only one person or one department in an account. Learn how your product may serve other teams beyond the CISO like the CIO, general counsel, CMO, CFO, CDO, CPO, VP of infrastructure, CEO, the board, etc. And get to know each of them. If you don't know them, they surely don't know you.

- Find the gaps in your closing process. Seek help from your manager and senior sales leaders for feedback.

- When a sale closes, the work begins. Invest time in your customers for long-term relationships.

CHAPTER 8

RUNNING YOUR BUSINESS LIKE A PUBLIC COMPANY

*"If you sincerely want to change your life:
raise your standards. What changes people is
when their shoulds become musts."*

—Tony Robbins

I ONCE HAD A FRONT-ROW SEAT to an amazing sales performance that is a great lesson in grit and determination of a Tech Sales Warrior.

At the time, I was working alongside a technology partner sales rep who was still relatively new to his organization. We were both selling into the same company, but our deals and budgets were different. He'd received a verbal commitment on a deal with a company but hadn't been able to close it.

He was doing well at his firm, but he hadn't yet had his breakout moment. Day in and day out, his prospecting was on point, he was building relationships with resellers that led to valuable meetings, and he continued to study the markets so he would be at the top of his game. I had seen his presentations recently and they were efficient and to the point. Even though we didn't work directly together, we communicated closely on several deals.

To give you some more context, he was working for a public company. At public companies, everything is a little fiercer. The metrics are set higher, the deadline pressure more intense, the expectations more relentless.

This rep knew it was the end of a quarter, and that his team and his company needed the deal he was working on before the deadline. No one had to tell him that. When the final day of the quarter arrived and there was still no word from the CIO of our prospective client, this rep decided he was going to do whatever it took to make the sale happen that day.

What makes this particularly remarkable is he already had hit his own personal numbers for the quarter. Not only did he not personally need it, one could even argue he would've been smarter to let the sale happen the following week and get a jump on his quota next quarter. But a selfish mindset is the enemy of greatness, the enemy of a Tech Sales Warrior, and ultimately the enemy of the growth of a person.

Even with the warrior mindset, the odds were definitely stacked against him pulling it off. He wasn't feeling well, and the prospect's office was more than a two-hour drive away. He had to track down the CIO who never seemed to stop traveling. If he managed to do that, he also would have to establish himself with a new procurement team and lock down a budget that wasn't completely set. And he had to do it all within twenty-four hours if he was going to make the cutoff.

The only thing in his favor was a previous verbal commitment from the CIO that the sale would happen and the rep also had paperwork ready for a signature. But when he called the procurement team on the final day of the quarter they told him they had heard nothing from the CIO. Emails, texts, and calls went unanswered.

It sure didn't seem likely he'd be able to get this closed in time to get it recorded in the current quarter. The deal, the internal approvals, and the commitment all were due to expire that day. The CIO had told him to call his cell if he needed anything, but he wasn't picking up. None of his colleagues knew where he was either.

After driving for over two hours through a mini snowstorm, combing the office hallways for another two hours, and sitting in his car for one more hour in the cold parking lot, this partner and friend called me.

"I just got the purchase order! I was in the parking lot waiting for any sign of the CIO. At 3:45 I saw him walking out to the parking lot. He was waiting for a cab. I jumped out of my car, ran over, and of course tried to be as casual as possible." He chuckled at the scene as he continued telling the story.

"Wait, you ran up to the CIO in *a parking lot*?" I asked.

"Yes, I had too. I explained I wasn't crazy and was actually trying to help his firm get the best deal possible and solve their problem. I reminded him of his commitment and all we had done together to get this done," my partner explained. "Without a beat, he pulled up the two documents from his email and electronically signed them on the spot."

My partner added, "I thanked him like crazy as the snow was still falling on the both of us. I looked like a little snowman by the end of it. He then got in his cab and drove off. "

"Wow!" I said. "That took guts and courage. Congrats, man."

He finished off his story by telling me, "I've actually been waiting in my car for the last hour for the purchase order to process through their procurement team just in case something went south. But it just landed at our company." I congratulated him again on his success and told him drinks were definitely on me.

Wow. *That's a warrior.* He didn't think, "Hey, I already met my quota, it's a long drive, I'm not feeling great, it's snowing, and this CIO is impossible to pin down, it's out of my hands, I'm calling it quits." All of those would have made fine-sounding, valid excuses. But his manager, his company, and his shareholders needed this deal. He decided to hold himself to a higher standard. Months later he received a huge promotion and, without a doubt, a hefty raise to go with it. I'm lucky to know him.

There are essentially three kinds of tech sales reps and you get to choose which you want to be. And, make no mistake, it is a choice. It's not one you can make instantly and suddenly you're that kind of rep. It's a choice you make in your daily actions, and that choice plays out clearly over time. If you don't like where you are at, change your behavior. If you want to become and remain a Tech Sales Warrior, it's a daily grind.

#1–The Forever Struggling Rep. This rep dreams of quotas, but never hits them or maybe scrapes by one lucky year. There's always a reason or excuse for not hitting, of course: the lack of existing accounts, the market climate, the product, the cost, bad timing, the sun is shining, it's cloudy…you get the idea. Occasionally this person will have a decent quarter but for the rest of the year it's about "just barely hanging on." Many in this category eventually wash out because sales is "not their thing" or they hop around to a new company every year chasing a new salary or OTE that they never hit, hoping magically a change of circumstances will be their solution.

#2—The Successful Rep. This rep does fairly well most years and is comfortable meeting quota or just a bit more than quota. This rep follows some of the principles in this book, but occasionally lets standards slip. They may miss quota one year, but they usually bounce back from that miss the following year to stand on stage again. Reps in this category often get bored because they fail to challenge themselves and let beliefs about their limits get in the way. Some get comfortable with their current status, or let external factors block further success. So reps in this category are solid performers, but with a bit more attention to daily details, they could crush it beyond their wildest dreams.

#3—The Tech Sales Warrior. These are the reps who do whatever it takes, including driving more than two hours to sit in a parking lot until he can get the signatures he needs, and then is willing to wait another hour in the car to ensure all the details are finalized to book an order on the last day of the quarter. But Tech Sales Warriors also understand that the real work is the day-to-day grind, not just the spectacular sale. It's those extra cold calls on the day you don't feel like it. It's packing some of your days from 7:00 a.m. to 7:00 p.m., and then still taking a client out to dinner. Consistency. Ownership.

Getting it done. Nothing will stop them from hitting their numbers.

The warrior mindset sometimes means foregoing a holiday or time off. It means caring that your company needs the win even if it doesn't necessarily impact you. The tough part for some reps is understanding that greatness doesn't come easy. It involves daily sacrifices. Warriors understand there are no shortcuts—you have to do the work every day. Once you fully commit to this mindset, your career will go into full blossom and you'll be astounded by what you accomplish.

How do you get this mindset? It starts with understanding it's always your choice. You control the process, not the other way around. Once you implement what you learned in the first seven chapters of this book, you get to decide your level of success.

Quota crushers find ways to push themselves and learn to love the mental toughness that elite sales requires. I recommend this: run your own day-to-day activity as if you yourself were a public company and it was your responsibility to make sure timelines and metrics are always met. Hold yourself accountable that your customers are happy, receiving value, and renewing their contracts.

I see too many sales reps with a quarterly mentality. I'm not talking about trying to get a sale in before the quarter ends like in the above story. I mean that they don't set any daily metrics for themselves; they set goals in weeks or even months. Their process is rooted in the question: "What do I need to do to get by this quarter?" Or scoping out a potential path to quota versus ensuring it. And if they've already met quota for the quarter, they're fine with taking their foot off the pedal until the next quarter starts.

That's the kind of mindset that wouldn't cut it at a public company. Metrics and accountability are everything at public companies (and high-achieving private ones). You need to put this same kind of pressure on yourself. You should know your metrics and sales timelines day by day, week by week, month by month, all the way up to annual. Be relentless about it.

Another key aspect of the public-company mindset is incorporating the needs of the larger organization into your thinking and goal setting. If you put a deal in the queue as likely to happen by a certain deadline, it's now more than just you counting on that sale.

At a public company that is answerable to shareholders, this kind of thinking is ingrained. The accountability for not letting a deal fall apart and bringing it in on time is a huge focus, because the company has shareholders. And I'm saying those pressures are actually good, because they make you a better, more battle-tested rep.

Am I saying all deals will always be 100 percent in your control? No. I've seen deals that looked great at one point fail because a key champion left the company. Deals can fall apart because of sudden budgetary cutbacks that couldn't be foreseen. I've even seen deals fall apart because someone passed away.

The point is not that nothing can ever go wrong, and I'm not saying that determination can solve every problem, every time. But there's so much more that is in your control than is not. There are many more times that what could seem like a valid excuse—maybe even *is* a valid excuse—can be turned around and you can still land the sale, and on time. Count on the possibility of the yes, and then do everything you can to make that possibility a yes. Give it your all and then give more.

When you have this mindset and come through for the company again and again, you make yourself indispensable. Your company is NOT going to want to lose you. The pay, perks, and benefits will come your way. It pays off, but the tough public-company mindset has to come first. The rewards and recognition aren't instant, but they will come, I promise you.

As you go through you career, if your find yourself in category #1 or #2, you can always decide to change your habits and rise to category #3. It's within your control. The Tech Sales Warrior understands that each quarter and each year the score rolls back to zero. In many cases you'll have additional challenges: the quota will go up, the accounts may change, the market may be struggling, and customers will sometimes retire.

Yet the Tech Sales Warriors take complete ownership anyway. It's a daily process to maintain warrior status, where sacrifice and hard work are foundational. There will be tough days where things don't go as planned or your energy and health is not in a peak state to perform as you normally would. Tech Sales Warriors show up anyway and do what they can with whatever resources they have that day. Or sometimes they have to know when to take time to recover so they can get back to a peak state quickly.

The overall key takeaway is about taking true ownership. That means you don't look for excuses, however reasonable they can sometimes be. It means finding a way to get it done, charting that path, raising your standards, and holding yourself accountable as if you were the largest and only shareholder in your career—which you are!

And guess what? Holding yourself to that kind of strict accountability is not easy. It's why the elite salespeople are rare (and rewarded handsomely). If you're wondering if you can do it, the next chapter is for you. It's all about how to reflect, recharge, and renew in the face of the grind.

ACTION STEPS FOR CHAPTER 8:

- Decide how committed you are, because it's always a choice. Are you willing to hold yourself accountable and run your day-to-day like you are a public company?

- Check in with yourself on a regular basis. Do you start easing up when you've hit your numbers for the quarter or the year? How can you identify this and address this before it impacts your pipeline?

- Identify where your comfort zone limits you and what you can do to get better. Analyze your sales process and ask where you found yourself drawing back and unwilling to grow and get better?

- Do you extend your passionate commitment to success to include your company and colleagues? The best reps do.

- Identify one area in your business in which you could implement a small daily habit that will greatly impact your pipeline.

- Review past deals that have slipped. Could you have done anything differently to change the outcome?

- Decide what category sales rep you want to be every single day.

CHAPTER 9

THE 3 RS: REFLECT, RECHARGE, RENEW

---

*"Calm mind brings inner strength and self-confidence,
so that's very important for good health."*

—Dalai Lama

THROUGHOUT THIS BOOK, I've talked about the necessity to push yourself if you want sales greatness and a transformed life.

But operating at peak performance in the competitive world of tech sales eventually takes a toll. Being a warrior does not mean never taking a break. In fact, if you fail to find ways to reflect, recharge, and renew, it will catch up with you and you won't be able to maintain your level of performance.

The key is to find the balance in your life and what works best for you. Sometimes reps begin chasing the lifestyle they see other reps posting on Instagram, thinking that will make them happy and relaxed, but that's not always the case.

Volunteer work is not usually what comes to mind first as a way to recharge, but I have personally found it to be renewing. Of course, vacations or treating yourself to a luxury item may come to mind. Or maybe just dedicating a weekend day to doing nothing but enjoying your family is your best way to refresh. Those are all excellent; use any that work for you.

Figuring out what allows you to consistently achieve high levels of output will be an important self-reflection point throughout your career. What do I need to do to bring my best to my work every day? How do I prepare myself for the rigor of tomorrow? Is there something I need to take care of for others or for myself in order to ensure I'm more present and on my game?

I want to return to the idea of volunteering as a means to mentally recharge. It may not be for everyone, but it's power really came home to me a few years back when a customer, a reseller, and the firm I was working for all came together to clean a hospital facility that treated children with cancer. Our customer was a major health provider, and this was one of their facilities. For many of these kids, even a little dust could be dangerous to their health.

So when I say we cleaned together, I mean we CLEANED! I don't think there was a nook, cranny, or crevice that had a speck of dust when we were done.

This experience has stuck with me because I found it so energizing, and I could tell the other participants felt the same. The feeling of camaraderie and doing something useful for others was amazing.

We didn't do it for business purposes, but it did have a side benefit of bonding us even closer to the customer. It was just a natural byproduct of doing something good. It's more evidence that sales isn't about being selfish, sleazy, or deceptive (as too many people believe). Sales at its core is caring about others and wanting what's best for them. When you do that, the relationships and the money follow.

If you have an opportunity to partner up for any kind of volunteer activity with clients or resellers, do it. You won't regret saying yes.

It's also important to make a larger point here. One of the best things you can do to recharge your own batteries is give back to others, regardless of whether it has any work connection at all. There are literally millions of ways to volunteer your time and talents. Surely there's something out there that matches your values and interests. Even volunteering just once a month can be invigorating.

I find it refreshing because volunteering often gives you a sense of perspective and connects you to others. You can't clean a hospital for young cancer patients without recognizing that your work worries, however important they can sometimes be, are something you can handle. It may even help you work harder when you realize what a blessing and opportunity you have in front of you.

And even if you choose to volunteer in a less intense cause, the connection you create with others is invaluable.

Of course, volunteering is just one of the many ways to renew yourself. Let's take one step back and look at why a chapter on reflecting, recharging, and renewing yourself would find its way into a book about tech sales.

One of the messages I've been trying to hammer home is how hard you have to work if you want to become an elite-level tech salesperson who crushes quota year after year. While I've been sure to remind you of the financial rewards and the fun, I've also not sugarcoated what's involved.

In Chapter 3, you learned that you need to get in early and stay late (or be extremely efficient with your time and even then long days may occasionally be called for). There are no shortcuts. You also need to pack your schedule each day and be relentless about daily prospecting. No one is going to care more about your success than you, and that's why scheduled habits help you win. Then I upped the ante in the last chapter and gave you examples of digging deeper and taking complete ownership of landing deals, even when the effort required borders on the superhuman.

Yes, I want you to be a Tech Sales Warrior. Nothing feels better than the sense of accomplishment that comes with elite-level success, and I want that for you. So I won't lie about the work involved and the mental toughness it takes.

But no one can be superhuman indefinitely. Determination is good and even necessary, but relying completely on gritting your teeth all the time is not a smart strategy. It's a recipe for an eventual crash and burn.

That's why it's crucial to find ways to recharge so you can stand up to the challenges of being a top performer.

Staying fresh begins with day-to-day actions. The best thing you can do is set aside time for reflection every single day. First thing in the morning, have some quiet time. It could be five minutes, or it could be thirty minutes depending on you and your situation.

During this short reflection time, think about how you're going to set up your day and what special challenges may lie ahead. Some people like to meditate, do spiritual reflection, pray, or read something inspirational. As long as you set aside the time and make the effort, you'll find what works best for you.

I'd also recommend stealing a page from elite athletes and using the power of visualization to see yourself crushing quota. Envision the work, the habits, the day-to-day activities, the deals—everything that goes into making you successful and able to achieve what you need.

Use affirmations to confirm your strength each day in the mirror (e.g., "I am a top sales rep, I overcome great challenges by helping the world around me, I am a consistent prospecting machine, I love challenges," and similar thoughts).

However exactly you use this quiet time, the only thing you don't want to do is skip it and jump right into your day. It's remarkable how just a little bit of quiet reflection can make the day go so differently.

You also want to be mindful of your health. Some reps are real fitness hounds and have an extremely healthy diet. That's excellent. But if that's not you, that's fine. But you do want to at least make reasonably healthy choices. Exercise regularly, eat and drink moderately and sensibly, and manage stress appropriately. I have found that on the days where I get my morning workout in I have far more energy throughout the day compared to the days I miss. I've also found after a very stressful call or day, nothing helps fix it more than a great workout. Sweat it out!

Let's face it. A lot of the job is sitting, making calls, sending emails, doing client research, and attending meetings involving drinks and food. So you've got to plan exercise into your week or things can get ugly quickly. Our fast-paced schedules can also encourage grabbing quick, unhealthy meals or very long and lavish meals followed by late-night happy hours. You're going to lose the much-needed stamina if you neglect your physical health, and that will make you less effective.

You also may need to work in massages, stretching, yoga, and physical therapy to maintain peak performance. And never forget, nothing replaces a good eight hours of sleep. You need to find and maintain the right balance to keep yourself physically energized for your work.

This is a high-stress role, which can take its toll mentally, too. Keep tabs on your mental state and needs. Don't underestimate journaling daily as a way to stay mentally balanced. If you need to take a break every few meetings from using a camera, do so. If you need to take a day to do absolutely nothing or to attend to household chores, do it.

Also, make the time to stay engaged with family and friends. With an incredibly busy schedule, it can be easy to let those important relationships suffer. Don't. At the end of the day, this is what matters most, and if you neglect relationships, you may begin to question who you're working so hard for.

Finally, I hope you'll never be afraid of seeking outside professional help if it's needed. Your mental health cannot be overlooked or neglected. If journaling, meditating, breath work, praying, exercising, and eating good foods isn't working for you, ask for help. Your own HR may be a great resource. You could also consult a doctor or dietitian.

Another thing I highly recommend is doing a daily report of your work accomplishments at the end of every day. It's possible your manager already requires it of you. I never did one until I had a manager who started asking for one.

When I was first asked, I was already a successful rep consistently crushing quota year after year. And if I'm being honest, I was a little resentful that I was being asked, almost as if the implication was my daily activities needed to be monitored even though I was getting the job done and then some.

But it wasn't long before I came to love the accountability of the daily report, and the satisfying feeling of seeing what I accomplished each day and/or where I may need to pay more attention. It reinforced good habits because I reviewed them every day. And if I had a day without accomplishing what I'd set out to do, I could see that instantly and make sure it didn't become a regular habit.

The final thing I want you to do at the end of each day is set aside quiet reflection time. This is a bookend to the quiet time that kicked off your day, and my suggestions are similar: reading, meditating, journaling, breathing exercises, and similar activities. But there's one additional thing I want you to do every night: express gratitude for the day and anything good that happened in it. Choose three simple things—personal, professional, random. It doesn't matter what the category is. Even on rough days, you can find something to be grateful for. It's a wonderful way to end your day and sets you up for restful sleep.

Sometimes, though, the daily intensity begins to overwhelm, and it's time for stronger measures to renew. When you take a vacation, do your best to make it a true vacation. Get your work in enough order before you leave that you're not bothered all the time. Take the break. I've been guilty of this one and have learned that nothing gets me recharged more than truly breaking away completely from work to recharge.

Think about the trips you would find truly relaxing. You may not want to plan that Disney trip with the whole family as your refreshing trip. We all know there are some vacations that you come back from feeling like you need a vacation to recover from the vacation! I personally find visiting other cultures and learning about them very relaxing and enjoyable. I prefer extensive hikes in rugged terrain. You may desire a wine tour through Bordeaux. Choose what is best for you.

Treating yourself to luxury items can be a form of relaxation. I don't judge how other people relax, and I do buy myself nice things on occasion. But I do want to give you something to reflect on and that's this: in most cases, experiences make people happier than things.

That's been true for me and many of my close friends and family. A dream trip is often better than a fancy new car (and I like nice cars!). A hobby may give you immense pleasure, happiness, and a new skill in the process. A meal at a top restaurant or with your mom may be more rejuvenating than buying an even bigger television. Or maybe it's just having a meal at home with family. I'm not saying don't buy a car or a TV; I'm only encouraging you to be mindful about what you buy and think about the things that bring YOU true happiness and satisfaction. When you spend money to enjoy yourself, make sure it's something you actually enjoy!

A final thought for this chapter. If you remember that your job is to make your customers' lives better, it will help keep you motivated. Just like volunteering, keeping yourself directed toward the happiness of others keeps you more relaxed and less stressed. Take joy in what you do.

You're set up for amazing success now. But once you become successful, can you handle it?

ACTION STEPS FOR CHAPTER 9:

- Set aside quiet time at the beginning and end of every day to reflect on the day. Be sure to include things you're grateful for.

- Do a daily report for yourself, even if your manager doesn't require it. Did you accomplish your goals for the day? What do you need to focus on tomorrow?

- Find ways to volunteer and give back to others.

- Take time for yourself and treat yourself to things you genuinely enjoy. Experiences may have more of an impact than things.

- Care about the happiness of others and find a way to weave it into your work.

- Assess your eating, drinking, exercising, and sleeping habits. Does anything need to change for you to be in a peak state to perform?

- Make time for your family often.

- Meditation and prayer can help calm a busy mind.

- Find the balance that helps YOU perform your best.

CHAPTER 10

YOU'RE A QUOTA BEAST EVERY YEAR...NOW WHAT?

"Failure is not the outcome—failure is not trying.
Don't be afraid to fail."

—Sara Blakely

BEWARE OF BECOMING the "war story" sales guy with no recent wins.

Over the past chapters, the importance of continuous daily effort and measured results has been emphasized. The need for that daily work never goes away throughout your career. If you let the daily habits slip, you may become the "war story" sales guy.

I've seen versions of this persona many different times in my career. A veteran sales rep with a multidecade-long career arrives at a new company and enjoys sharing his work history with anyone willing to listen.

How he was number one rep at X Corporation a few years running. How he closed millions of dollars in business over his career. And on and on. But somehow, no new opportunities come in this current role, no meetings, no trials, no revenues. He points the finger at his inside rep, the marketing, the product, anyone he can. He takes no ownership.

Look even closer and you'll notice these types of sellers no longer have interest in prospecting at all, and certainly not daily prospecting. They are above it now. And what they end up with is no pipeline and no revenue.

This is what happens when you forget the mindset of a Tech Sales Warrior. If you're only living on past success, you'll only ever have past success. A Tech Sales Warrior understands every day counts and takes ownership of that their entire career.

There's a different but related problem I often see with young reps who've tasted some success. These reps are hitting quota almost every single year, usually somewhere around the 120 percent range.

Often these reps have developed a superb close rate, as much as 80 percent. What happens is they start relying on that high close rate and cut way back on prospecting. Even though they've worked hard to improve their skills, they're staying in the same income bracket as they were prior to increasing their close rate. If they simply remained focused on daily prospecting and kept that improved close rate, they would launch their income into the stratosphere. They could be hitting quota two to three times over.

What's going on here? Do the old war story rep and the young rep on cruise control have anything in common? Don't get me wrong, they may be content with their new way of life, and if that's the case, that's definitely their choice to make. But the old saying "Nothing great ever came easy" is absolutely true. As humans, we strive to grow, and we do that by facing huge challenges and overcoming them. That makes us better, stronger, and more fulfilled.

When a rep is slipping or throttles back the effort, I think the root problem goes back to the fundamental motivation of Finding Your Why that we talked about way back in Chapter 1. One of three things is happening:

- These reps never took the time to find a deep purpose to keep them motivated.

- These reps had a Why, but it now needs some more reflection and updating.

- These reps still have a good Why, but they never revisit it, so the fire has faded.

I know all about this because I personally experienced it after a couple of years of crushing quota. I felt like I was starting to lose my edge. Crushing quota wasn't as exciting. In fact, it was easy because I had the processes down cold. Sometimes after the student loans are paid off, and the financial freedom is happening, the wonderful trips around the world are taken, and the cool gifts to yourself, family and friends are enjoyed, you begin losing your inner fire. And then you begin to lose your way. For me, revisiting my deep purpose was what I needed to keep crushing quota.

I also encourage you to remember the opportunity you have in tech sales. Many folks would like to be in your shoes. As was mentioned in the introduction, you're in a career that opens the door for you to earn right alongside the top lawyers, doctors, and even some pro athletes.

Think about this comparison. The average rookie in the NFL made about $610,000 per year in 2020. And the average NFL player has a three-point-three-year career. Over the course of your career, you can blow those numbers away. This is an elite opportunity and if appreciated properly, it offers you and your family amazing possibilities. Do you show up every day like a pro? Do you put in the work like a pro? Do you deliver like a pro? The glamour and the goods go to those who do the work that others aren't willing to put in. Think about it and let it fire you up!

SHOULD I STAY OR SHOULD I GO?

There's no shortage of opportunities after you become a Tech Sales Warrior. A rep who can bring millions of dollars of business year after year will always be in extremely high demand.

You'll also be building strong relationships with lots of people outside your company as a normal part of your work life. The chances to change jobs will be there.

Of course, there's no way I can give you a strict rulebook for when to move on and when to stay at your current company. Individual circumstances vary too much.

However, I can give you some general guidelines to consider. The most important thing is to take the long view of your career and to be very intentional about your decisions. The case for moving on to another company usually makes itself. It's more money, a step up in the hierarchy, or a chance to extricate yourself from a challenging situation.

But before you just leap, here are some things to reflect on before saying yes to a new company.

- Too much jumping around and many short stints at companies will begin to make people wonder what is going on. Remember back to the "You Are a Brand" chapter. What story are you telling if you move around a lot? The short one- to three-year stints can put a bad mark on your résumé.

- If you're getting an offer for an immediate On-track earnings raise with a new company, that doesn't always mean that long-term you'll end up ahead. Remember the grass isn't always greener. At the new company, you may never hit more than your base plus nonrecoverable draw. What may seem like a nice bump in immediate pay may actually cost you more in the long run (think commissions and hitting quota 2x, 3x, +). The longer you stay with one company, you also tend to reap more extras like real stock, better titles, access to bigger accounts, and other benefits that can be enormously significant. Don't forget the intangibles like internal reputation, flexibility, trust, a strong supporting manager, a well-developed understanding of the market and products that take years to master, a proven market, and having an established pipeline. All this can be hard to quantify but key to long-term success.

- Beware of chasing title inflation as a sales rep. At the end of the day, the Tech Sales Warrior is here to sell. Whatever they call you—account exec, sales rep, regional sales manager, guy with a phone—it shouldn't matter. We are here to sell. Don't forget it. If you believe a title change helps in outreach, by all means work with your manager on it, but I find it silly—the customer isn't fooled.

- You should also realize that the longer you're at a company, the more you'll understand how to mesh client needs, the company needs, and your needs. It's at the intersection of all those needs where truly sustained success happens. That takes years of work to build and grasp. Your knowledge of company products and initiatives deepens over time, and the company will rely on you when putting together more complex quotes and deals. You'll soon find yourself an extremely valuable asset to the company. The more you're valued, the greater the rewards. Something to think about before changing jobs!

- Do your homework. Ask sales reps working at the company and/or your partners what they know about the new company. Read up on industry analyst articles and news about the company. Is the market sustainable? A growing or dying business? Too soon or too late for the markets?

- If you're offered stock at a startup or pre-IPO, take time to understand it. Ask a financial professional if you don't. Overvaluations, lofty ambitions that don't stand a chance, and dilution due to investment that will never be paid back will all greatly impact your chances to ever receive a dollar. Understand the risk you are taking on. Lofty Wall Street overvaluations can actually mean less money for you and can create targets that are very hard to overachieve on. Companies doing endless funding rounds without purpose aren't always a good thing for your pockets.

- Avoid jumping to your immediate competitors. Not only can it create legal issues if there are noncompetes in place, it can hurt your personal brand when done poorly. What does this say about you to your colleagues and your customers that you just sold the competing solution too? Situations arise and circumstances may be different for you, but choose this path with extreme caution.

- Finally, bring the choice back to your Why. Will it be served with this new company? Am I really giving everything I can in my current role? Are there other roles at my current company that I could still grow in? Does this change really have anything to do with the company or is it more about me and a need to spend more time working on myself outside of work? Or spending more time with family and friends? Or needing a hobby?

None of this is to say never move. It's only to say consider it carefully and make sure you're not caught up in the moment and just chasing shiny objects. Look deeper at the offer and at yourself.

FINAL THOUGHTS ON YOUR JOURNEY

I'd like to leave you with some final considerations about handling success and your adventure ahead.

Stay away from negativity, particularly on social media. That's all just noise that can only distract and hurt your reputation.

You'll likely see examples of this with certain prospects who like to bash sales reps on sites like LinkedIn. In some cases, you can quietly learn something if the prospect has a legitimate complaint about the prospecting style of a sales rep.

But whether the complaint is legitimate or not, don't become involved in commenting or liking the post yourself. That's just a waste of time and a way to damage your own reputation.

Similarly, be very careful about your retweets, likes, or shares. For example, in cybersecurity, I've seen sales reps posting stories about security breaches that paint the breached company in a bad light. Without thinking about it, you might share that and then it looks like you're willing to gloat about another company's problem for your own benefit. Be mindful of what you post, and be careful what you share or like on social media.

If you're ever tempted to sink down into this kind of negativity, remember this quote by George Bernard Shaw: "I learned long ago, never to wrestle with a pig. You get dirty, and besides, the pig likes it."

Your focus should never be on whether other sales reps at other companies are doing a slapdash job. And it shouldn't be calling out companies publicly. Your focus should be on how you can get better. How can you educate your prospects about the true cost of their problems and what the solution is? Your mission is to focus on customer value; everything else is just noise.

As you become a quota crusher, you'll sometimes run into haters, doubters, and trash-talkers. And during rough stretches, that hater or doubter can take up residence in your head.

When that happens, I think about a story I heard about a crow biting the back wings of a bald eagle. Rather than waste energy fighting off the crow, the eagle kept his focus on flying higher.

Soon the crow could no longer breathe at the heights reached by the eagle, and the crow tumbled to his death.

Be the eagle. Focus on climbing. Laugh off trash-talking or

negativity that is thrown at you. Move forward. Stare down projections and then crush them. Smile. Concentrate on your daily prospecting, booking meetings, closing deals, and delivering value. Let your numbers speak for you.

Every single day counts. Follow the process laid out in this book and you'll become a Tech Sales Warrior.

ACTION STEPS FOR CHAPTER 10:

- If you find yourself letting success slip away, or setting your efforts on cruise control, revisit your Why.

- Be wary of jumping jobs without giving it a lot of thought. It can be smart to move in some cases, but you should reflect on the benefits of staying with your current company for the long term.

- It takes years to become a master seller of any product or service. Remember that, and invest your efforts accordingly.

- Reflect often on your personal brand and your Why.

- If you're considering a new job, make sure that's what you want. Sometimes the change you want is something else. You may need a hobby or more time with friends and family, or want ongoing education.

- Make yourself irreplaceable with your results, but never let yourself believe you are irreplaceable.

- Avoid noise, and continue to focus on how much value you deliver clients.

- Ignore haters and doubters. Be the eagle and keep climbing.

CONCLUSION

I REMEMBER A CONVERSATION I once had with a young rep about a self-help book I'd recommended to him based on a problem he was struggling with. Had he read it?

"Yes, I read it," he told me. "It had a lot of good stuff in there."

"Did you implement any of it?"

"Well, no," he admitted, as he looked down. Then he paused, and added, "I guess that's what you're supposed to do with it."

"YES, that's what you're supposed to do with it!"

I was having a little fun needling him about his failure to take action. And he was appropriately sheepish about his failure to do anything with what he learned. He later shared he had read many business books, but struggled to take the time to implement the new solutions learned. We laughed a little bit more, but then refocused on the gap.

I advised him to pause on certain chapters and do the work that is called for. It's okay to start small. Implement bite-size changes daily and you'll see results.

The point here is a serious one. The failure to implement proven strategies can be the difference between getting fired or having the career of your dreams. It can be the difference between scuffling along and worrying your whole life or achieving mastery and complete financial freedom. It can be the difference between being perpetually stuck and having a major breakthrough in your process. It can be the difference between barely achieving quota and absolutely crushing quota year over year.

Taking action is what matters. No doubt you may read a self-help or business development book that you don't agree with or see the benefit in, but there are many out there that you will. The problem is often less with the advice and more with the readers. Too many people are consumers of content. If you say, "I read this and I watched this and I learned this," that's only the first step. But what have you done with that knowledge? How has it served you? Enhanced your life? Changed your life? Use the tools that have proven to work for many.

Being excited about this book and feeling good when you finish it means nothing by itself. The truth is many people will close this book, understand that these are proven strategies, get enthusiastic, and then...do absolutely nothing different.

Commit yourself to be one of the people who does the hard work of implementing something new. Sure, you'll make some mistakes and take some lumps. Come back to the book and figure out what you can do better. But keep going. Cultivate mentors and learn from the best in your company. Prospect daily. Take ownership of your numbers, your pipeline, your revenue, your relationships. Always be a student of the game. Focus on your daily outputs. Commit yourself to the way of the Tech Sales Warrior and I guarantee your life will change.

Once you crushed quota, the even harder part is to consistently crush every year after. With the Tech Sales Warrior mindset, you'll be equipped to face those uphill battles every year.

There will be tough days, deals lost, and you'll often feel the weight of the grind. Remember to check in on yourself, physically and mentally. Find ways to constantly motivate yourself and spend time with your Why. Shake off the rough days with a workout or a day off. Don't forget to have fun.

And remember the power within you and the opportunity before you. You do have the ability to change people's lives—businesses, communities, individuals. Live in that. The efficiencies your solution provides may save and create jobs, give time back to your customers, reduce stress for thousands, and be an overall force for good in the world.

Your personal impact has the possibility of being profound, too. I've witnessed a sales engineer who delivered meals to her cancer-stricken customer. A sales rep who built a presentation for a CIO over the weekend so the CIO could enjoy a soccer game with his kid. A sales team raising tens of thousands of dollars for disabled veterans. A sales rep who spent a weekend day with his client, because he was lonely. A rep who spent his vacation building schools in an impoverished area. Reps who become close friends with customers and attend their weddings. A sales rep and engineer who hopped on a call at midnight on a Saturday because their client was facing a cyberattack. A sales rep who raised over $100,000 for sick children. A sales team who spent their weekend cleaning up a trash-littered beach.

These are some of the many stories you don't hear on social media about amazing work by sales reps. The world needs more Tech Sales Warriors. Rise above the noise. Choose your impact.

An amazing life is completely within your control. In the words of the great Michael Jordan, "Nothing of value ever comes without being earned."

Take action. You can do it. Believe it. I'm rooting for you!

Let me know how the journey is going. If this book helped you at all, send me a note; I'd love to hear about how you are implementing it. Email me at techsaleswarrior@gmail.com or connect with me on LinkedIn at linkedin.com/in/chrisprangley.

Note: I primarily use LinkedIn for networking and selling the products and technology I love (yes, I'm still in the trenches with you), not as a forum to share sales tips. If you have any questions, emailing me at techsaleswarrior@gmail.com is the best option. I will do my best to personally respond in a timely fashion.

Go get 'em!

ACKNOWLEDGEMENTS

THE OLD SAYING "It takes a village to raise a child" is ever true when writing a book. Over three years of preparation, over a decade of practical application, and over three decades of learning have brought me to this point. Writing a book while working full-time is a marathon of sacrifices (the 4:00 a.m. kind) but a rich learning experience I'm grateful for.

There have been many people who have impacted my life and helped me along the way, taught me wise lessons, and supported me through this book journey. I'd like to call out a few specifically:

For my entire Varonis family, thank you! There's hundreds of folks to thank over the years. I'm appreciative of every one of you. My journey with you has been fruitful, a master class in its own right, and a wonderful personal and professional growth period of my life that keeps getting better. From finance to legal, customer success to support, R & D to marketing, incident response to forensics, technical training to channel, professional services to sales ops, administrative support to TDR you've taught me a lot! And it is your hard work and efforts that make everything possible on the sales side.

I want to especially thank Yaki Faitelson for giving me the opportunity to lead, reminding me that every day counts, and motivating me with the long-term vision. For Guy Melamed for his financial wisdom and creating vehicles that work for both the business and the sales force. For Jim O'Boyle for inspiring me with his dedication to craft, and still being the first in the office after many decades in the game. For Greg Pomeroy, for continually distilling what matters most, and for giving me my first opportunity in the field of IT sales. For Sam Wethje who always believed in me, pushed me to climb to unprecedented heights, and ensured we had a lot of fun in the process. For Patrick Fleming and Jeff Kane for the ongoing help and insight.

For my DC team who was there from the start, and will always have a special place in my heart in the world of sales and as friends. How you have picked up the torch and run with it, crushing quota, strengthening partner relationships, and delivering massive value for customers, makes me smile. Bravo! I want to especially thank Justin Wilkins who showed me the extraordinary power of a sales engineer early on in my career—always willing to go the extra mile to serve a customer—how powerful a disciplined SE can augment the sales process to drive quicker results, thinking outside of the box, and being by my side through years of adventures on planes, trains, and automobiles.

And for my amazing West Team—you fire me up every day with where we have come, and where we are going! From TDR to channel, inside rep to customer success, SE to SR, to managers and beyond. I'm so thankful for each of you, and enjoy the enthusiasm and effort you bring to your work every day. We are building something truly special in the entire industry and I look forward to doing that every day with you. Thank you!!!

For my Scribe team who helped put all the pieces together and bring this idea to life. What started as a goal to impact a handful of struggling sales reps for the better turned into so much more. It has been a thrilling ride! A special thanks to David Moffitt who has been a pillar throughout this journey and helped get words to paper. Many thanks to Sarafina Riskind, Skyler White, Brian Phillips, Cristina Ricci, Barbara Boyd, Tucker Max, JeVon "JT" McCormick and the rest of the Scribe Team for bringing this all together.

For my formal teachers over the years, in particular, Richard Burns (Good Counsel, MD), Rich Seel (Good Counsel, MD), Br. Bob Arrowsmith C.F.X (Good Counsel, MD) Dan Vaillancourt, PhD (Loyola Univ. Chicago), Mine Chinar PhD (Loyola University Chicago), Fr. Jerry Overbeck, S.J. (Loyola Univ. Chicago), and Terry Knickerbocker (NYU, William Esper Studio, TKS)—who collectively taught me critical thinking across literature, history, economics, philosophy, performance, spirituality, introspection, the joy of lifelong learning, and a growth mindset. Thank you!

For past, current, and future customers—who have shared their secret challenges and goals, worked together as partners on a joint mission, and who have taught me rich lessons in how their businesses operate, thank you! What an honor it has been to be included in your projects and careers. A special thanks to Matthew Radolec whom I had not only the honor to sell to, but eventually work alongside with and learn from while assisting new customers.

For my resellers, partners, and strategic integrators—what an awesome trek together. I'm so lucky to have had the experiences I've had with you all. It's always more fun with you, and we've gone so much further together. Thank you for your trust, the opportunities, the friendship, the knowledge, and the many great meals and adventures together. It's been an honor to grow with you and your families. Looking forward to these continued amazing years ahead!

Special thanks for the years of ongoing support and motivation: David Gibson, Brian Vecci, Dana Shahar, Rick Proctor, Caroline Kinlin, Rob Sobers, Josh Tays, Laura Ellen, Laura Johnson, Ofer Margalit, Mark Wilcox, Dov Gottlieb, Rich Haddad, Thor Lynch, Courtney Chau, Kara Kruk, Stephen Frethem, Louis Casale, Jordan Parsons, Paul Dietz, Jonathan Biederman, Jason Johnson, Gilad Gam, Ofir Ronen, Linor Havia, Shai Cohen Golan, Itsik Ben aderet, Aaron Beveridge, Sagiv Elmaleh, David Bass, Gilad Raz, Jacob Broido, Alana Brenner, Snir Ben Shimol, David Asraf, Maor Kallner, James Spencer, Alex McEwan, Thomas Zaki, Bryan Dreyfus, Jason Bonasera, Dan Hatter, Ian Friedman, Steve Tassinari, Parker

Gaines, Zach Franklin, Michael Wallace, Thomas Zaki, Kristina Rith, Judith Athelstanlowe, Raphael Kelly, Ryan Clement, Ryan O'Boyle, David Smith, Jared Hale, Damien Brodie, Caitlin Jans, Derek Keen, Kristen Kosich, Brett Edelen, Alex Beardsley, Forrest Temple, Joshua Smith, Rocky Savage, Mike Opper, Steve Cohn, Leah Clause, Matt Lock, Jerome Soyer, Matt Mariner, Michele Neuberg, Brandon Lapetina, Anat Weiss, Meital Gordon Yachin, Belinda Ng, Gerry Olmedo, Jonathan Thomal, Chance Hoover, Damien Brodie, Bryce Paulson, Rich Letter, Pete Carroll, Chris Massa, Bob Krzysik, Brandon Wilburn, Jesse Rosenbaum, Frank Martinez, Samantha Mcmurray, Kevin Crowley, Eduardo Jimenez, Michael Ross, Henry Sosa, Jacqueline Weiss, Ginny Wieland, Allegra Tatusko, Mara Reichelscheimer, Tony Secret, Linville Thao, Jeff Sheaffer, Mark Lipscomb, Thomas Simpson, Chris Olsen, Hilary Forman, Claire Dawson, Jennifer Maldonado, Abby Prescott, Steven Rennard, Nick Sakmar, Kaitlin Skamarak, Bo Lambert, Amanda Blezard, Hannah Schemoul Kaizer, Trevor Stilphen, Jim Tunell, Jamie Arestia, Ryan Derryberry, Bryan Popa, Inessa Rozenberg, Avia Navickas, Aviram Elad, Jarrett Levin, Justin Lubman, Jacqueline Biggio, Mark Hoffman, Jordan Talbot, Ben Lui, Chris Schuh, Gary Comitto, Daniel Moya, Michelle Ruden, Illya Branzburg, Ashley Spinelli, Manuel Roldan-Vega, Matt Skelly, Sydney Burns, Christopher Hoesly, The Palladino Brothers, Alexa Kusovitsky, Patrick Lynch, Amit Cohen, Greg Jarvis, Michael Barreiros, Agnieszka Schwarz, Julie Duffy, Rebecca Jing, Rachel Hunt, Mason Takacs, Jonathan Pistilli, David Derksen, Aaron Koning, Sag Baruss, Bob Denney, Brooke Bowman, David Jenkins, Rotem Tsadok, Ivan Topalov,

Judith Athelstanlowe, David Leung, Daniel Callahan, Leon Hester, Jeremy Milton, Kyle Ziegler, Hila Aroch, Noy Barzilay, Carl Groves, Jamie Armitage, Tal Karlin, Brian Capalbo, Brian Keefe, Randy Frank, Austin Jewell, Kilian Englert, Kyle Vale, Elena Khasanova, Matthew Kelly, and the many more I missed…

And thank you for the partnership—Jennifer Eslin, Pete Chancellor, Brett Newgaard, Lester Bonnet, Andrew Roberts, John Manchester, Mike Kemp, Dwayne Gilliam, Dan Molina, Drew Harris, Steve Jung, Matt Estes, Nate Bishop, Jim Kebert, Matthew Ghering, Jason Dauer, Billy Stowe, John Karle, Andy Shulman, Mike Jin, Skip Goodwillie, Jeff Kelly, Mike Vergis, Jessica Burgess, David Jain, Scott Riser, Frank McLallen, Mark Gonzalez, Matt Ewart, Grace Joseph, Mark Miller, Susan Washo, Nate Phillips, Leon Miao, Pat Marsden, Jeff Smiley, Garret Pederson, Mandeep Singh, Brittani Neff, Ben Crist, Julie Tabot-Hubbard, Matt Kropf, Steve Tatusko, Matt Uvena, Ryan Priem, Pat Marsden, Ratna Chakka, Swadesh Guchhait, Nicholas Polychronopoulos, Alex Ortiz, Ed Martinez, Ali Tehrani, Ted Pibil, Joe Bennett, JD Mccormick, Brittany Anderson, Mike Eaton, George Wilson, Jason Scott Sr., Mike Conway, Nash Hickman, Chris Cairy, Curtis Eshelman, Tony Pirrera, Nate Phillips, Niko Alexiou, Sam Cattle, Tim McCauley, Ladd Parrish, Rich Douros, Michelle Lapuente, Ted Gagnon, Darren Cathey, Rich Lindberg, Timothy Grelling, Richardson Dubois, Emily O'Carroll, Steve Jarosinski, Sam Freels Salazar, Karen Swain Prosser, Andy Calvert, Ernest Dunn, Alisa Castro, Robert Graves, Andy Bernard, Matt Hillmark, Peter Dietrich, Ruben Navarro, Michael Hartman,

Cindy Monroe, Brian Hamill, Brittani Neff, Anthony Meoni, JP Garvin, Mike O'Hehir, Bob Justus, Todd White, Lamar Forehand, Patricia Malek, James Crifasi, Michael Hartman, Navneeth Naidu, Mike Heinmuller, Louise Finn, Rick Proctor Sr., Casey Andrews, Bill Murphy, Kurtis Kreh, Jacques Lopez, Ernest Dunn, Mike Korwek, George Cocoros, George Henderson, Libby Enochs, Jeff Bittner, Jake Jansen, Craig Callinan, Patrick Outlaw, Mark Salop, David Thomas, Collin Stoddard... and the many more I missed.

For my mother and father, Anne Marie and Patrick, who taught me the value of hard work and so much more: follow your dreams, keep the faith, help those who most need it along the way, and remember your blessings. Thank you for cheering me on my endless business ventures in yard sales, mowing lawns, door-to-door magazine sales, painting houses, billing for movie nights, chocolate sales, lemonade stands, and with all the pursuits in sports and the creative arts. Mom and Dad, thanks for always believing in me; for pushing, not fixing; and for always being there to pick me back up so I could keep going. I'm eternally grateful for your sacrifices.

For my sisters who have been my pillars throughout my life and a constant source of inspiration and counsel. For Katherine, you amaze me every day with your daily actions to get better in life, family, fitness, and business all while making time for others. For Dianna, whose courage, empathy, and discipline in the pool and out has wowed me for decades. For Laura, your creativity, no-fear attitude, and adaptation to new environments is amazing. And for

Caroline who has ventured all over the world, started over, and resiliently succeeded in multiple industries! Just wow, love you!

For David Liola who took the time out of his busy schedule to connect me with his IT sales friends and helped me find a path into the world of software sales and cybersecurity when I had no clue what I was doing. For Jeremy Birns, who actually hired me into my first role as a TDR in software sales when no other software firm was taking a chance. For Gigi Schumm, Bob Schumm, and Chris Schumm for opening my eyes to the software sales biz from a young age. For Brian Cunningham, who pressed me to leap at an opportunity when it struck. For Adam Abramson, who shared his journey alongside mine and helped me stay focused on the long term. For Mark Maready for the ongoing support. For Mike Reynolds who took me under his wing and showed me the value of face-to-face business transactions, long-term relationships, and showing up on time.

For Lauren Celinski, just for being you.

For Jason Beans, for giving me a view into the life of an entrepreneur, highlighting the importance and impact of sales, buying a meal when a broke college kid needed one, and offering me my first opportunity at selling in B2B.

For Eric Stone, who taught me the value of a dollar, real work, pushing oneself past the comfort zone to get the work done, and for giving me the happiness of one of my first jobs.

For my grandparents, who taught me the beauty of both the extrovert and introvert, serving family, faith, giving back to the greater community to make the world a better place, and that freedom is all a blessing that many before have sacrificed for.

Thank you to Dana Patrick Photography for the author photo!

For the hospitality industry, especially Morgans Hotel Group (now sbe Entertainment Group) and W Hotels for sharing the concept of WoW and exceptional customer service experience.

For the Upright Citizens Brigade, Groundlings, and Second City Chicago for ingraining a "Yes and" mentality and a strong focus on active listening.

For the clarity: Napoleon Hill, Dale Carnegie, Dr. Wayne W. Dyer, Marc Benioff, Tony Robbins, Philosophy, Ben Horowitz, Steven Pressfield, Sara Blakely, Guy Raz, Phil Knight, Morgan Wooten, Tim Ferriss, William Esper, James Allen, Jocko Willink, Gary Vaynerchuk, Viktor Frankl, Suze Orman, James Martin S.J., Robert Kiyosaki, James Clear, Elon Musk, Cal Ripken, Kobe Bryant, Michael Jordan, J.K. Rowling, Ray Dalio, Stephen King, David Mamet, Sanford Meisner, Paulo Coelho, Jim Rohn, Derek Sivers, Dan Millman, The Jesuits, Steve Harvey, Earl Shoaff, Ian Schrager, Jim Carrey, Les Brown, Pat Tillman, Travel, Barbara Corcoran,

Mark Cuban, Jeff Bezos, Daymond John, the Arts, Warren Buffett, Walt Disney, Antoni Gaudi, Faith, Tyler Perry, Frank Lloyd Wright, Brian Tracy, Julia Cameron, the Great Outdoors, Tom Brady, Roger Federer, Zig Ziglar, Matthew McConaughey, David Goggins, and Norman Vincent Peale...

To anyone with a dream and willing to do the work to make it come true.

And to all my friends and family, for all of the support and companionship over the years, thank you!

I look forward to seeing you all in the field.

—Chris

Want to share a story, note, question, idea?—email me at techsaleswarrior@gmail.com

Want to connect with me? Find me on LinkedIn at linkedin.com/in/chrisprangley

ABOUT THE AUTHOR

WITH MORE THAN A DECADE OF SALES EXPERIENCE in the enterprise B2B market, Chris Prangley helps global firms solve challenges in data security, collaboration, threat detection, and governance. He has a proven track record of overachieving customer expectations while building successful sales teams known for cultivating strong relationships and surpassing quotas. As the VP of Sales-West for a multibillion-dollar cybersecurity firm, Chris is a frequent speaker at industry conferences. He graduated from Loyola University Chicago with a BBA in marketing and a minor in philosophy.

Printed in Great Britain
by Amazon

17625033R00120